COMMON *Threads*

EMPOWERMENT

by Dr. Shellie Hipsky

The Missing Piece Publishing

United Kingdom   United States of America

The Missing Piece Publishing

Seathorne Walk

Bridlington

East Yorkshire, YO16 7QP

England

For information visit www.themissingpiecepublishing.com

Book & Cover Design by: Jennifer Insignares: www.yourdesignsbyjen.com

Edited by: Kirsty Holland: www.graceinthesun.com

File Formatted by: Bojan Kratofil

ISBN: 978-1-51360-424-4

Common Threads: Empowerment

is dedicated to my parents:

Libby Jacobs,

You taught me by example how to be an empowered woman.

Dr. Jack Jacobs,

Your work ethic and love are a part of who I am forever.

Thank you to all the amazing people behind the scenes from the "Mommy Army" of transcribers to the fabulous backers through Kickstarter who believed in *Common Threads*. To Neil Haley for being at the beginning of Empowering Women Radio and to all the wonderful ladies who helped with my TV show Inspiring Lives with Dr. Shellie.

To my fabulous Inspiring Lives team especially Brittany Ann Comer, Samantha Barna, Erica Menendez, Christine Marie Scott, Beth Shari, and Chanice Lazarre.

Thank you to the Missing Piece Publishing Team including Jennifer Insignares, Kirsty Holland, and Kate Gardner. To my publicist Jennifer DeCosta from Dash Public Relations for taking Inspiring Lives to the next level.

Thank you to my angel in heaven, Clarel Radicella, for your guidance and friendship. I am bracing myself and you were right, it is bigger than I ever imagined.

My family is my world so thank you my darling children Jacob and Alyssa Hipsky for being so great while Mommy wrote night and day. Thank you "Mr. Ken" for being so supportive.

My heart is filled with gratitude for the Global Sisterhood of Empowering Women for sharing with Empowering Women Radio your fantastic success secrets.

Thank you also to the amazing woman reading this book right now. It is because of you, that I was driven to manifest this project to empower other women internationally.

To Do List

---◆---

Feel:
- ☐ Empowered
- ☐ Loved
- ☐ Accomplished
- ☐ _____
- ☐ _____

Let Go Of:
- ☐ Resentment
- ☐ Jealousy
- ☐ Past Hurts
- ☐ Limiting Beliefs
- ☐ _____

Attract:
- ☐ Your Sisterhood
- ☐ Positive Vibes
- ☐ Good Energy
- ☐ Opportunities
- ☐ A Mentor
- ☐ _____

Visualize:
- ☐ Paying it Forward
- ☐ Your Happy Family
- ☐ Travel Destinations
- ☐ Dreams Come True
- ☐ _____
- ☐ _____

....

Notes to Self:

I need to take some time for myself in a bubble bath or curled up on the couch reading Dr. Shellie Hipsky's *Common Threads: Balance*. It is based on interviews from her *Empowering Women Radio*. I want to learn from mentors like Lucinda Cross who went from federal prison to being on the Today Show as a vision boarding expert. Melanie LaPatin from TV shows *Dancing with the Stars* and *So You Think You Can Dance* seems to have manifested more than dance moves. I also want to see how I could help world-wide initiatives like Hasten Patel's in South Africa who leads Power Circles for the next generation of Empowering Women! I deserve some Me Time!

Table of Contents

Chapter 1:
Shift Happens

My doctoral student said I needed "Shift Happens" on a bumper sticker because I have not only experienced so many dramatic life shifts over the years, but I have now come to expect them. While I know that they will be uncomfortable moments in time, I realize that they will bring the next beautiful chapters of my life.

Iris Dankner:
Holiday House

We sat perched on a white settee in the beautiful room that Iris Dankner designed. This room in the Holiday House represented a bridal suite in honor of her daughter. I interviewed this icon of interior design about her mission to raise funds for breast cancer awareness.

An eighteen-year breast cancer survivor, Iris created Holiday House in 2008 as the first designer show house held in New York City to benefit a breast cancer organization. Recruiting top interior designers, the show house is located in a historic mansion on the Upper East Side of Manhattan. The Holiday House has been endorsed by some of the most celebrated global luxury brands. The inspiration for their room design is based on a special life moment or holiday. Each room is decorated as a celebration of life.

Iris explained, "At age 40, at my first routine mammogram, I heard those dreaded words, 'You have breast cancer.' I had a 5-year-old and an 8-year-old, and my world turned upside down.

"That was probably one of the hardest days of my life. I asked my kids to sit down. Oh, I could cry now. I asked them to come in and I said, 'Mommy wants to talk to you.' I told them, 'Mommy has breast cancer. I'm going to need some surgery, but I'm going to be fine.' And I explained a little more, and then I said, 'Do you have any questions?' and my 8-year-old, who was a little older, said, 'Are you going to die?'

"I was so afraid, but I knew I had to reassure her. And I said, 'No, Mommy is not going to die. I'm going to need some surgery and then I will be fine. I might be slowed down for a little while, but I'm going to be fine. Nothing to worry about.' And I said to my younger daughter, Nikki, 'Do you have any questions?' and she said, 'Yes, can I go back and watch cartoons now?'

"It wasn't until years later that she was able to tell me how bad she felt that she couldn't process what I was saying. Children can absorb only so much. Talking to them and being honest was so helpful. They saw me volunteering and they started doing events with me.

"Nikki said that helping me is what finally helped her heal and feel better. She no longer wanted to feel guilty that she wanted to watch TV. At the time, she just couldn't hear more about what was going on with me.

"Fortunately, early detection saved my life. I vowed after the doctors put me back together that I was going to do everything I could to raise awareness, fundraise, and to help find a cure for this deadly disease.

"My dream was to have an event that combined my two passions: my love for interior design and my passion to eradicate breast cancer. I came up with the idea of doing a show house so that designers could showcase their work and we could raise money for the cause.

"Doctors helped put me back together physically. Emotionally, though, what helped me get back together was giving back. I met so many women that helped me go through my crisis… women who I would never see again. Nurses who held my hand during horrible moments. I wanted to pay it forward, and that's really how the journey started."

Iris told Empowering Women Radio about organizing a powerful photo shoot. "I found as many brave breast cancer survivors as I could and then they asked friends. You have to have courage to get totally naked and be photographed, and you have to want to participate. One of my friends asked a 27-year-old she knew. Her mom came with her to the photo shoot. The photographer was such a doll. He made us all feel so comfortable.

"While shooting the young woman, the mother was talking to our photographer and said, 'I'm a breast cancer survivor, too. I actually lost my mom to breast cancer, and my sister.' He said to her, 'You should be in the picture, too.' And with that, she took off her shirt. She held her daughter. He got the most incredible photographs.

"The mother said to me, 'That moment changed my life.' She said, 'First of all, I didn't want to let go of her.' The mother said she felt the guilt and the fear and the hope, all at one moment, and she started to cry.

"I told her, 'You know what, there are different ways you can help people.' Raising money… I think is just the icing, just the cherry on top of the cake. Helping women and helping them cope and be hopeful is the real beauty."

Iris Dankner explained the rules for the interior designers who display their work at Holiday House. "First and foremost, you have to be a really nice, happy person to be a featured designer. The Holiday House is so positive. It's a trickle-down effect. It comes from me and then from the designers. I say, 'Every once in a while, a diva slips by,' but there's a positive attitude here from the men and the women.

"My success with Holiday House, I think—fortunately and unfortunately—is due to so many people being touched by breast cancer. It's become such a success because so many people are affected. It warms my heart when people come up to me saying, 'My mom (or my aunt) had breast cancer,' or 'I am a survivor. Thank you for doing this so I can give back.'"

I asked Iris what survivors could do to lessen the blow of dealing with a traumatic medical situation such as breast cancer. Iris suggested carrying a journal. She told Empowering Women Radio, "It was a great help to carry my journal with me in the doctor's office. It's something to do when you're waiting for them to come in, you're sitting naked, and it's freezing cold. You are thinking, 'Why are they keeping me waiting?'

"It was great help to always have a journal with me. Still, to this day, I go for my mammograms. Eighteen years later, I still need a mammogram for the other side (I had a mastectomy on one side), so I still bring that journal. That's one helpful thing.

"Another positive move is let your friends help you. I think I was so used to helping people and taking care of everybody that it was very hard for me to let people do that for me. What I found out was, it helps them to help others."

Nan Cohen:
News Radio KDKA and Nan on Divorce

Nan Cohen is "The Divorce Expert." I interviewed her on Inspiring Lives with Dr. Shellie on TV, and she gave fantastic advice for the audience. Then I was on her C.B.S. radio show broadcast on News Radio K.D.K.A. I really opened up about my own life story and revealed more to the world than I ever had about my personal life.

It was after these powerful interactions that a deep friendship was formed. So when I realized that time had come for me to get a divorce, I knew that Nan was the person who could coach me through it. She went into high gear after our teary-eyed phone call. Nan Cohen assembled the right team for me and my little family that covered professionals to take care of our legal and emotional needs.

Nan has the resources to be a great divorce coach, and now she is even helping singles find true love by bringing the Dinner For 8 program to our local area. Nan explained to C.B.S., "People want to be social. They want to be out." By having dinner with eight eligible singles, people get to know each other in a relaxed settling without the pressure.

Nan explained to Empowering Women Radio her complex role as a divorce coach, "You get to the point where a lot of people (whether they're in long-term marriages or short-term marriages), they are just truly suffering. When you're suffering, you think sometimes you've got to always do that in silence. It is important to know you don't have to do this by yourself.

"People think that with a divorce, once they have an attorney, that's it. It's true that you can't do it without an attorney. Sometimes, though, you need to implement other people in the process who can get you the results that you need.

"At the time, you would rather do the legal work, but lawyers are not there to deal with all of the emotional stuff. Therapists deal with the emotional stuff, but they're not always with you side-by-side. It is what happens in an office versus the outside world, so I'm always bridging that gap for the individual going through the divorce.

"I'm changing the lives of people every day. My biggest passion has been for children. I recall one case in particular when a woman was going through a divorce and the emotional highs and lows of that stress. Sometimes it plays out on the children. It's innocent because you don't even realize that it's happening.

"I remember a woman who was positioning herself with her child by making her a new best friend, instead of realizing she was the parent in this situation. Once she realized where that was headed, we corrected the problem. Now she has a dual role of being friends with her children and being their parent. And so those are the things that I look for. The outcomes are just tremendous."

Nan provided suggestions and strategies for women who may be going through a divorce or those who are conquering obstacles in their lives.

Nan started with how she defines success. "I think success is always self-measured. I say it's on your own timeframe. I'm a goal-setter, and whether one's going through divorce or not, you've got to be able to set goals for yourself. Success just doesn't happen upon you. You've got to take it within yourself. Decide where you want to go with it. Then really look back and give yourself the kudos along the way for it.

"Divorce can take you to a really bad place. I always say, 'I'm blessed.' Unfortunately, I see people at their worst times of their lives, but I get to see them when they're through that process. It becomes the best time of their lives; that's how I really measure my success every day. That's why I keep doing what I'm doing.

"You have to realize that nobody can do this but you. I can give you all the tools that you need, but you have to empower yourself to make it happen. We can't do it any other way. Know that we're by your side. But eventually, you've got to be able to find it within yourself, become empowered, and get where you need to go.

"Never forget. Take those broken pieces with you. Always carry them. It's okay to go back and remember it. Yet, you must always keep going."

Nan knows about the pain of divorce firsthand. She shared her personal divorce story with my TV and radio audience. Nan's story is also written about in her book *Dealing with Divorce: Reality Revealed.*

She considered marriage a lifetime commitment. Unfortunately, that concept was shattered when she returned from a family vacation to her husband's demand for a divorce. It was the early 1990's and she was the mother of a 14-month-old daughter. Her world was turned upside down. Nan's husband (armed with knowledge from his prior divorce) accessed and emptied all bank accounts and closed her credit cards. He left her without even enough cash for a new car seat for their growing toddler.

The reality that Nan experienced included a long and bitter divorce, social stigma, joint custody, and emotional turmoil. Through it all, she gained empowerment by being there for others experiencing divorce.

Nan has been has been remarried 19 years and her beautiful daughter gained a great stepfather.

Nan Cohen explained why she works with people. "Taking time to make a difference in somebody else's life benefits you. And you know me with my famous line, 'Success measures differently to all of us.' Once you find your version of success, take the time to share it with others.

"Women are a powerful group. I think that when we come together, there's just no stopping us."

Heather Watkins:
Divas with Disabilities

Heather was promoting a segment for my Inspiring Lives with Dr. Shellie TV show. She was featured in a "What's Inspiring Me" segment when Divas with Disabilities was born.

Heather explained to me on Empowering Women Radio, "It was that one-minute YouTube video that I posted in a Facebook group page that my now-partner saw and said, 'Oh, my goodness, would you like to get together and start something new?' Dr. Donna R. Walton had been thinking about something like this for a while, and I had been, too. I hadn't seen anything like it in the Internet or through researching. So when we got to talk, it slowly evolved to become Divas with Disabilities. The organization showcases the talent and abilities of women of color with disabilities through various media platforms to help shape the perception of what disability' looks like."

Heather spoke about the power of the TV show, saying, "I think Inspiring Lives is a global movement showcasing greatness in the world. Many substantive people are make contributions. Your show has mobilized those efforts to bring about showcasing greatness in everyone. Watching Inspiring Lives with Dr. Shellie is beyond inspiring.

"Every time I see a new show, I'm thinking, 'Wow, it's just that one little decision that somebody made to enhance the lives of not only themselves, but also everyone around them.' The radius of impact is grand. I just think that kind of effort needs to be duplicated many times over. I'm glad that you have a forum such as that."

I asked Heather about important women in her life. Heather stated, "I often say that I'm book-ended by great women (my mother and my daughter), so I'm in the middle of them and I watch just how they have made decisions. My mother is setting the bar, and then my daughter is being empowered and inspired to walk her own path. That's what I love. I always wanted to make sure that she wasn't a mini-me, but she was like a big she, so she was doing her own thing. Those two are my biggest inspirations.

"My daughter is 19. She just wrapped up her freshman year at Emanuel College, and she is studying business and loves music. She's always trying to trying to form a new beat. She loves to put together rhymes, so she's very musically inclined."

I loved that Heather picked people from her own family. I hear that very often when I ask people who is empowering in their life. I can easily look to my own wonderful mother, Libby Jacobs, as an empowered woman, and my grandmother, too. My grandmother Lieutenant Hilda Nevin Miller was honored with a Bronze Star as a nurse in World War II. It seems to be a trend that many women who are empowered then pass that legacy on to their family, and I certainly am working to do that with my own daughter.

Presenting positive images and perspectives on women with disabilities is vital to Heather because, "Growing up, and looking through magazines or just watching a television show, there weren't a lot of strong images played out in the media of people who were different. In developing Divas with Disabilities, we wanted to advocate across the board. We keep in mind that people with disabilities are varied folks. I think in that respect, it's important to not have one person speaking for many."

"We didn't see these images across the media landscape, so this was our way of exercising creative control. We formed a network so that women of color who were differently abled had an online place where they could connect with other women who had cross-disabilities. We have divas who are amputees, or who have (like myself) muscular dystrophy. They might have MS. They might have cerebral palsy. They are across the country—L.A., New York, Atlanta, in the D.C. area—and the momentum is taking off now globally. There really is an excitement about it, so I'm happy to be involved in this kind of movement."

Heather explained the effect that having muscular dystrophy has had on her everyday life, "I think there was a time in my life when I felt like it was eclipsing my whole being, my whole story. Then, over time, what I realized is that having muscular dystrophy is one part of who I am."

"I started to put that into perspective and thought, 'Wait a minute… this is a detail. It doesn't stop me from doing anything. I just have to adapt things.' Once I had that shift in perspective, it was really the catalyst for my advocacy.

"Also, as a parent, I thought about what I wanted my daughter to see. What kind of legacy did I want to leave my daughter? When I started seeing myself as more of a whole person instead of like a lesser entity that was when I felt like my whole life just took off.

"Muscular dystrophy more than shaped my life; it has transformed it. I see the gift in having a disability because I can see it from kind of a comprehensive view, instead of just a little part of it.

"There is a gift in no longer seeing the world as just a closed-off space. It is now not a place that I fear. Once I realized that having a slowed-down life means that I actually see more, I say that I'm a 'slow walker' to see more, literally and figuratively.

"There was a time when I felt like the world was just a huge place that I was afraid of because I was always afraid of falling. Now I don't see it that way anymore. I feel like, 'Okay, you just have to adapt to whatever you want to do and you can get to your desired goal.'

"I see it as a gift now, because I see both sides of it, seeing how both sides serve me. Having a disability doesn't mean that that's the end of your life. It just means life's going to be adapted in a different way."

"Focus on what beneficial impact you can have. I think that is a good starting point: just to assess who you are, where you want to go, and have a bit of a plan. Have a goal list. They don't have to be huge goals. Start with five things that you want to do in the next year.

"I think you should really just consider everything that you want to do and not look at yourself as just being this small person that can't make an impact. There's that saying that, 'A mosquito can bite you, but it has that little edge.' So it's tiny, but it makes an impact, doesn't it?

"Don't think of yourself as being so small that you can't affect change. Any little thing that we do can definitely help others. There are so many people who stand around us who can be affected by change."

Chapter 2:

Collaboration, Not Competition

I have been so blessed with incredible connections with women business owners, young women, and amazing mothers around the globe. Women can lift each other up and support each other. On the flip-side, they can look through the green-eyed lens of envy and miss out on beautiful connections and successful collaborations.

We are living, working, and often mothering in a day and age where we can see everyone's highlight reels online. We can attend huge networking events in person or listen to podcasts such as those archived on Empowering Women Radio. There are many ways to retrieve information and connect with ladies around the world. The question is, "Will we utilize these tools for finding joy and success?"

Lisa Chuma, who was the Editor-in-Chief of the Inspirational Woman Magazine based in London, UK, offered this advice to me during an informal conversation: "Women should complete each other, not compete." Let's learn from the women of the world what barriers there are, and then what connections can be made.

Natalie Cerino Kovacic:
The MomCon

The MomCon brings together a tribe of mothers who are willing to share the triumphs and struggles that come with motherhood. The women talk about parenthood, careers, and relationships. They discover what their version of "having it all" looks like. This conference was created to inspire moms to go after their goals, to rediscover their creativity, and to remind them that children are not the only members of the household who should grow and learn.

I had the opportunity to interview Nicole Mildren and Natalie Cerino Kovacic, co-founders of the MomCon, in tandem for Empowering Women Radio. Natalie Cerino Kovacic discussed her career path changing: "I was clerking for a judge, and I found out I was expecting my son in 2010. I was just starting my career. I was a year out of law school, and my husband and I, all of a sudden, were like, 'Oh, my gosh. We are having a baby.' We were not expecting that at all.

"I wanted to work for years before I had a child. So here I was, faced with this decision: do I work full-time and have this newborn at home? I'm a new attorney. How can I really make it jive? How can I make it work?

"I felt a need to put it on hold because I wanted to stay at home with my newborn son. I did. For that first year, I felt really isolated. I went from having these intellectual conversations, working on interesting things, being around adults all day, to changing diapers and whatever.

"I wasn't from Pittsburgh. I don't have family in the area, and I just felt that when I went to play groups, it was like all we talked about was feeding schedules and diaper changings, and nobody was talking about the real nitty-gritty stuff of motherhood, like the obstacles and how hard it was. I just felt like I was the only one who felt this way.

"I was coming from a huge Italian family; every Sunday dinner was a major event. And even through law school and college, I always loved planning and organizing events. They were a lot of fun for me, so I said, 'You know what? I'm going to organize an event that I would want to go to as a mom. An event that would make me empowered in my mothering and parenting. It is okay to have my own goals and dreams. I can go after them!' So, that's what I did.

"I created this event at the end of 2012. I was at a women's conference and I saw these women coming together. It was really amazing, but I said, 'Why don't we have something in Pittsburgh for moms? We're in business together, but, like, what about all the obstacles that mothers uniquely face?' That is exactly what we're doing here.

"Now we're in our second year, and it's amazing. My full dream of meeting women who are like me has completely come true. The conference is packed with amazing, incredible women doing just great things with their kids, communities, and businesses. It's awesome."

Nicole Mildren: Champagne to Crayons

Nicole is the Marketing Director for the MomCon. She has been a marketing and advertising consultant for over a decade. The judging of mothers is something that has happened for generations, only now we have the virtual world to see what everyone is doing behind their closed doors. Nicole has insight from the marketing and mommy-blogger perspective.

Nicole Mildren created "Champagne to Crayons," an interactive blog where "Moms come together to celebrate life, motherhood, and everything in-between. It's a non-judging place. So, you can come there and not feel judged."

I asked Nicole Mildren about this phenomenon and what mothers are judged on the most. Nicole explained that it is not just one thing. "It's how we raise our children. If you breastfeed, if you don't breastfeed. If you feed them organic food or not. You're judged on everything you do, so I just tell moms, 'Do what you believe in your heart and what is best for your family, and go for it.' Moms are down on themselves every day because we compare and we say, 'Hey, this mom is doing this, and I'm not.' Don't compare yourself to other moms, because you don't know what's going on with them. You don't know the whole story, but do what's best for you, your family, and your kids."

Natalie Cerino Kovacic was a lawyer by trade, and she now works as an entrepreneur and co-founder of the MomCon. She said, "Our generation is the first generation of mothers who grew up with social media. Our mothers did not, and I think that poses a unique obstacle, and the 'Facebook Effect,' or whatever it's called, where you're more likely to portray all the good things. Women are just bombarded with that all day, every day, from other moms.

"There was a great article in the Huffington Post the other day about a mom. She said something along the lines of, 'I posted this picture on Facebook of my family and I flying a kite, and you would have thought it was the happiest day of our lives. Well, what you didn't see was, it started raining five minutes later and the kids were crying, and one of my kids pooped his pants.' She said it was actually a horrible day. It looks nice, but it was actually a terrible day, you know, and I think that's what it is. We have to deal with that, whereas our mothers did not.

"Another thing that is unique about our generation of moms is that a lot of us are more educated than our own moms. We're not only more educated, but because of the Internet, we've been exposed to a lot more, so we want more. We want to travel. We want to be spontaneous."

Nicole explained who influenced her: "My mom is a true inspiration to me. She was a stay-at-home mom for 16 years and then went back to work. I realized that I didn't really want to do that. I love my mom. She's my best friend, but I didn't want to stay at home for 16 years. I wanted to know what my dreams were and kind of live them out.

"Fortunately, my husband has encouraged me to live out my dreams. Regardless of whether it's your husband, your significant other, whomever it may be, I think that it's huge, because if someone else believes in your dreams, you believe in them more yourself… You're able to accomplish more when someone else is pushing you and saying, 'Hey, honey, you're doing a great job. Try it again.' He's your personal cheerleader just for you."

Nicole stated, "I was actually a single mom. Dave, who is my husband now, and I were not married when we had our daughter, and that's a big story for me. People judged that. There are a lot of people who are out there that that happens to. years old, but I was a single mom for a little bit. You can do it. I think being a single mom drives you even more because you want the best for your child, and you want the best that there is out there. I think single moms are way more powerful than married moms. I 100% believe that and I give them all the credit in the world.

"The MomCon is all about empowering yourself as a mom. Not about coming in and learning how to breastfeed. It's not that kind of conference. It's more or less for if you're in a career right now or if you want to start your own business. It's learning how to empower yourself, create time management, eat healthier while you are a mom, and create your own business. So, truly, it's for any mom. It is for moms who want to create their own dreams while becoming empowered."

Stephanie Barnhart:
Football, Food, and Motherhood

Stephanie Barnhart, the New York Editor of Mommy Nearest and author of the blog "Football, Food, and Motherhood" is interested in building a community of mothers and women through her blogging. She pointed out that, "Moms are very strong. You go through this whole birthing process, raising toddlers, and sleepless nights. But you can't do it alone because that can become mental anguish. I think the whole aspect of community is why blogging is so big and important these days. It's not a journalist who is writing an article. They are moms who are speaking from the heart about issues that are highly affecting them.

"I meet some people, like, on social media who I have never met in real life. You have this connection. We actually had a conversation in one of our groups where a mom asked, 'Is it weird that I'm going to meet up with a mom that I met on Instagram at a play date?' I was like, 'It is absolutely not odd.' I feel like you probably know that person better than you would your own neighbor, because Instagram is like a gateway to her life, and it's her honest feelings and how she lives her life. If you are connecting and you like how she's raising her child, the chances that you are going to be friends is probably a lot higher than just someone you really don't know who lives next door behind closed doors.

"I think it's cool to be able to empower each other in this whole new level of virtual villages. It's great. It helps you through it.

"When I started my blog, I felt so alone and I didn't know what to do because I didn't have friends who were pregnant. I was in this huge city. Being able to openly talk about it, then have people actually read it, and then tell me they feel the same way... it's very heartening. It really is."

Stephanie wrote a powerful article for the Huffington Post titled "Mom Shaming Trends That Need to Stop Now." She reflected on this newer phenomena, "The sad part about my article going viral is that so many people shared it and it went viral because so many people are affected by mom shaming. I think we really need to just put our priorities into understanding that, we need to raise our children just to be happy instead of worrying about each other and keeping up with the Joneses so much."

I know that many of my listeners and readers would like to learn how to create some extra income through blogging. When asked for tips about this, Stephanie said, "I think the one word that describes how to make money is authenticity. I'm an accidental blogger. I did it because I really wanted to talk about what was happening in my life. I didn't go into it with the thought of making money. I honestly didn't think about that until it started to come. I think that the best way to start monetizing is to just write about what you really want to write about and to just be yourself. Share things that other moms are going to be able to relate to, because that's what people are going to connect with, and that's what's going to make you money.

"Blog readers want to learn about you, want to see your life and how you're handling it, because they're either living vicariously through you or they want that connection and to know that they're not alone. And that's the selling point. That's what we all want: that connection.

"I just heard Diane Von Furstenberg talk the other day. What she said was that the greatest thing about being your own boss is that you're the one driving the bus. She is right. You're in charge and you're building your own destiny. It's all about your own confidence, and you make the rules. If you want to make a million dollars, go get it... make a million dollars. If you want to just make enough to pay your rent and be able to spend every day with your son, then that's an amazing goal. Being able to understand what you want to get out of it is what's going to empower you.

"Every mom wears a million hats, and it all started when I was pregnant and I was in New York. I didn't know anybody who else was pregnant. All my friends were back in Pittsburgh. They didn't have kids and I didn't know what the heck I was doing. I decided to write about it, because I always wanted to be a writer.

"I thought maybe it would be kind of funny to write about all these weird things that were happening. Daily, I was dealing with the big belly in New York, riding subways, or trying to get through Times Square. It just kind of took off from there. Then when I was six months pregnant, I lost my job, and New York is not a cheap city to begin with, so I was like, 'What am I going to do?'

"I was doing some social media on the side through tech consulting. My friends who actually had their own businesses in New York were like, 'Why don't you just find a way to be able to stay at home and turn it into a business?' I had never even thought of that.

"And I didn't realize how actually easy it is to become an entrepreneur. I mean, there are a lot of steps to it. But the overall business plan and trying to just actually get there and, like, make yourself an LLC is really quite easy. It's the American dream. It really is. It's the new dream.

"So I said, 'All right, I'll give a shot.' I didn't have a lot of expectations. I didn't say, like, 'Oh, I'm going to get all these investors and I'm going to make millions.' My goal was really to just be able to stay at home with my son and to make enough to be able to pay the rent and to justify not going back to work.

"In New York, daycare can cost up to $40,000 a year, and … so I was like, 'What am I going to do, go and just try to get a job that's even paying $50,000 or $60,000, and paying someone $40,000 to take of my son?' That didn't make sense. I would rather just stay at home.

"From there, it was just easy because I was at home with my son. I was really happy. I was doing everything that I loved and it just kind of grew. It was spread through word of mouth. I was able to do something I was really passionate about and just kind of turn that into a business. All my new clients always come because I've done such a great job. I think it's all about the customer service.

"I'm not this big, large company. I'm a person. I'm a mom. I can relate to a lot of people. I know how to help them get them gain their own voice out there, whether it's for their own business or themselves. We all help each other grow, and it's been great.

"I think like any kind of new mom, a lot of my best ideas come at like 3:00 a.m. You're like, half awake. You're watching some really bad infomercial and you start thinking, and you do that woman thing where you start making lists. I think when you're a little bit sleep-deprived, you get a little bit more creative. You're like, 'Oh, this could maybe be a really good idea,' and you just kind of learn to implement it.

"Also, being up late at a night and being a new mom, you look to see what other people are talking about and what the current issues are that mothers are dealing with. So you can really relate to your readers. I think the community of mothers is so empowering in itself. If you connect with them or find what their problem is and then you talk to them on that level, you gain their trust. It's an honest trust.

"A mother being able to connect with another mom, understanding what her issue is and being able to solve that for her, is empowering. You see a lot more of these little entrepreneurs coming up. We're able to be able to stay at home with our kids, but we're able to still provide an income and feel valuable. We are doing it all. It's possible. I'm proof.

"Women sell themselves short. For instance, I just had a talk with my one girlfriend. She's starting her own business up in the Hudson Valley and she wants to do all these great things.

"When I talked to her about what she was charging people, I was like, 'What? You're giving it away for free? You should be charging this amount of money. You need to know your value and stick to it. You're worth it and the right client will pay it.'

"And now my friend is really working towards it. That is empowering. I like to see her grow, and she supports me back."

Chapter 3:

Vision

I have guided so many friends and mentees in the vision-boarding process. I can recall teaching about it in Skyping into South African power circles. I taught the little ladies with big business plans through the Princess Entrepreneurs group my daughter attends how to design their future. I wrote about vision boarding in Tarra Flores Sloan's *Manifest It All: Because Why Not You?* and Betsy Chasse's *The Missing Piece of the Law of Attraction*. Every time I think about vision, I can look to the fabulous changes in the ladies lives whom I have taught this and my own transformation!

Simply looking around my new dream house with the cars in the driveway and the designer shoes in my closet to proves to me that it works on material things. Yet, it's the sleeping happy children, my new supportive husband in the other room as I write, and this book series you are reading that make me 100% positive that there is magic in seeing your visions clearly and manifesting them into reality!

Lucinda Cross:
Activate!

Maybe you have seen Lucinda Cross on Dr. OZ, the TODAY show, or read about her journey in *Essence Magazine* that took her from jail to media darling. She is always impeccably dressed and helping women internationally activate their lives. Lucinda Cross is the "Chief Activator," best-selling author, speaker, and spokesperson. She is known as the go-to girl for taking massive action. Ultimately, her work is about helping women live a life of fire, fun, and freedom.

Lucinda explained to Empowering Women Radio that, "In college, I made some wrong decisions. I was trying to take success in my own hands. I ended up in federal prison.

"I came out and found myself into a bad relationship, and we had children. I got into a relationship looking for love during my transformation. I was vulnerable with an open heart. I accepted a relationship that was less than anything that I deserved.

"During this whole process of being a single mom and ending the engagement, I started my business. I just took my two babies and decided to care for them in order to regain my life back. I said, 'I did not go through prison and everything that I've went through to get into a relationship that feels like another prison.' Not at all; I had to make changes.

"I made the decision that there has to be more to life. I always wanted to believe there has to be more than this. I strive for more and I always say, 'There's more to life than this situation, more than what I'm seeing.' Sometimes all you have to hold on to is words like, 'I can do this,' 'I love myself,' or 'I am enough.'"

Lucinda Cross explains why she activated her life, "I'm afraid of just not doing what I'm called to do. I don't want to end this term that I have, not completing my calling. That's what's driving me is to know that I have an assignment to do. I have a calling and a purpose. I'm not going to stop.

"The process of vision boards... I love it. It's something that I use to help to transform my own life. It's a tool. It's a medium to really connect with someone else and kind of bond. I do it with my children. I'm still pulling at my husband to work with me on one. He's like, 'Oh, just put down what you think we need, you know, put down where you think we should go.'

"But vision-boarding is really allowing yourself to be creative, to go back to that free, young little girl or little boy who once had these dreams and visions of pink unicorns and flying off of buildings. It's allowing yourself to really be free to put down those things that scare you in a positive way to say, 'I can become that, and I can do that.'

"Vision-boarding allows you to be free to dream again and give yourself permission to say, 'You know what? These are the things that I desire. I'm not going to allow what I don't see to stop me from getting them.' It helps to focus your mind, priorities, and goals to go after. Then you can run in hot pursuit towards your dreams.

"For me, vision boards are where you can go every single day. You look at it to say, 'You know what? This is what I'm going to work on. These are my goals right in front of me.' It's a fun exercise of creative visualization. It's part of the Law of Attraction. It's a part of really just speaking life and attracting the things that you desire in life and being awake when they arrive and open to receive them.

"I want you to be selfish and greedy with your love. You can start seeing your future unfold. Do not allow yourself to be a part of anyone else's agenda.

"This is your time to love on yourself. This is your time to be greedy. This is your time to say no to other people's agendas and timeframes, and their situations, and for you to choose yourself first. Invest in your own love, peace, and prosperity."

Christine Marie Scott:

Clever Crow Consulting & Design and Nosetouch Press

Christine Marie Scott explained how we connected. She says it was pure, "Serendipity. Our mutual friend, Jacqueline Bitting saw that Dr. Shellie had need of a graphic designer's services and referred me to her. We set up a meeting, and from the first moments of talking to one another, it was clear that we had kindred energies, with lots of enthusiasm and natural understanding.

"I am a freelance graphic and web designer and brand consultant, operating under the name Clever Crow Consulting and Design. I assist my clients in developing their brand by analyzing their current branding efforts, discussing their core values and vision for the company. Then I take that information and translate it to an impactful visual identity that both informs and attracts the customers they are seeking.

"I am passionate about branding and design, and I love to provide entrepreneurs and small businesses with the marketing tools they need to help them achieve their goals. I admire and relate to their enthusiasm, drive and vision. I find it fulfilling to contribute to their company's growth.

"Books are another passion of mine. I love to read them and I love to design them! I am a partner in a publishing company called Nosetouch Press. We publish works of science fiction, fantasy, horror and mystery. It was created as a reaction to both a shared love of the printed word and classic design, and also because we saw a lot of speculative fiction anthologies out there that needed good design. My partner is a published writer and an editor, and he tackles the words, while I concentrate on the book design and layout. We work together to market it on the Internet—it's very much a digital dance we do."

We found through discussion that Christine had gone through a divorce. She gave insight into the pain of her marriage. "Being in a relationship with a narcissist is a spiritual death by a thousand cuts. Narcissists are on their best behavior at first. They appear to be supportive and appreciative and they seem to understand you completely. They'll appear to value your empathy and compassion. They appear to approve of you, and this can be dazzling at the outset.

"Once you're in the relationship for a while, and they've gained your trust, the escalating attacks will begin. You accept them as being valid because you love them and believe that they are trying to help you because they care about you.

"The attacks become more frequent and more personal, as do the demands they make of you—and later, you realize that they are intended to sap you of your self-esteem, to keep you in a position of dependence and vulnerability.

"Then comes the rage. This is combined with threats, wild accusations, constant blaming, and irrational demands. There is "gas-lighting" which is intended to make you doubt your own eyes and thoughts by making you appear to be the emotionally imbalanced one.

"The ever-changing, self-serving rules. The pathological lies. They'll tell you you're worthless, that not even your family loves you, that you can't do anything right—and that only if you follow them without question can you be on the right path.

"It's like walking through a minefield... only they've put the mines all around you, and insist that you follow them through it. They tell you that you're worthless and they'll expect you to be grateful for their tolerance of your ineptitude and for their 'support' in spite of it.

"It's like being in the company of a tyrant. You find yourself utterly bewildered, emotionally bruised, and full of fear, doubt, shame and guilt for everything you do. Part of you knows what they are telling you isn't true, but under the relentless onslaught you endure, you fear that maybe it is.

"Inevitably, you start to believe that you are broken, worthless, incapable, weak, unlovable and utterly alone— with only the Narcissist as your salvation. By this point, they will have systematically isolated you from your external support system, so the only mirror of yourself that you have is your abuser—until you no longer recognize who you are, anymore. You become a stranger to yourself.

"Narcissists are masters of manipulation and deception, and by the time you begin to see the truth of who they are, you are physically, emotionally and spiritually drained to the point of collapse.

"Some people never escape a narcissistic relationship. The lucky ones, like me, have someone come into their life that recognizes them as they were, before they were drained of their spirit. It's like a new mirror and when you look into that new mirror, you see and you remember who you really are. It's a life-changing moment, seeing your true reflection again. Who you were is almost a stranger to who you had become at the hands of the Narcissist.

"You regain hope, and even though you cannot imagine how you can possibly escape the Narcissist's manipulative maze, you begin to quietly make plans for escape, anyway.

"Hope gave me strength. Hope revived my will. Hope renewed the well of my spirit. True friendship, understanding and love helped me find my way out of the labyrinth I'd helped build to placate the Narcissist.

"The escape from my marriage was long, painful, expensive and absolutely terrifying. There were days that I didn't think I could hold on, moments where I feared I would lose it all.

"I had spent so many years learning to comply, to be silent and to question nothing. To make myself as small and inoffensive as possible to escape notice that every step

I took out of the relationship felt awkward, frightening and unreal. Through it all, however, I began to rebuild my external support system and they kept me from sinking, kept me on course. It took me a while to be able to deal with people without feeling the sting of constant judgment, and to be able to stand up tall again.

"Now that I am out of the relationship, I understand that Narcissists expect you to be nothing more than a reflection of their own false and inflated self, and that you must relinquish your own identity to do so.

"I realized that my ex was actually a hall of mirrors. I had become lost in an ever-shifting maze of fractured and distorted reflections of him at every turn. I never knew where to turn or what was real. But there was an exit, and through the loving help of friends and family, I found my way to it and became free.

"I have a most special man in my life who gifted me a lovely and delicate pearl pendant. I treasure it for several reasons. One of the reasons is that I immediately could see the pearl as a metaphor of my own life, and an inspiration to keep going, to never quit working to build the life I desire for myself and my family.

"Pearls are created when a grain of sand intrudes inside an oyster. It irritates the oyster, which then extrudes nacre in an attempt to soothe the discomfort. That nacre builds up over time and the pearl is ultimately formed. Without that irritation, the grain of sand remains a small, non-descript grain of sand, nothing more. I saw myself as that grain of sand. Layer by layer, I become more lustrous as a result of the challenges I have faced. I value and appreciate those layers of experience that have made me into the woman I am, and the woman I will become."

Christine Marie Scott explained how women can overcome their fears and create a vision for their future, "The first step is honest self-reflection. Determine where you are strong and where you are weak. Look at your failures and figure out exactly why you failed, forgive yourself for making the mistakes you made, then do whatever you need to do to ensure that you will not make those same mistakes in the future.

"Accept that you are not perfect and never will be, but that is okay: know that there is never a perfect set of circumstances from which you will 'start over' or 'launch your new life.' After that, think about what you want your life to be; not what you (or others) think it 'should' be, but what at the core of your being you know will fulfill you and make you happy. It doesn't matter how illogical or unattainable it might seem to be. Hold fast to that vision. Protect it. Nurture it. 'See' it happening in the future, and act on that vision.

"Action is essential; just thinking about it isn't enough. Any action in support of the achievement of your goals advances you closer to them. The small steps will eventually lead to small successes, and those small successes will compound. You will gain confidence in your abilities, satisfaction in your progress and through that, you will find that you have the strength to face those fears that were originally keeping you stuck in place.

"I find than when I remain mindful of my thoughts, keeping them goal-focused, positive and backed with productive action, the cosmos delivers results, large and small. Sometimes those results simply make me smile, other times they make my jaw-drop. I love that."

Christine described how she un-officially mentors younger women, "Growing up, I was never in want of love or comfort, but I did suffer from a lack of guidance. While I am endlessly grateful for those people who loved me unconditionally, I realize now that I also needed people in my life sharing their own practical experiences with me; people who could demonstrate that each of us has the power to help ourselves. Someone who could have helped me learn to make better choices in my life, or help me recognize that not only was I talented and worthy of success, but that I had the intelligence and the ability to make my dreams a reality.

"I knew I was valued by those who loved me, but I lacked the confidence and belief that I had worth in the world at large. I was uncertain and unprepared, emotionally and practically. As a result, I enjoy being able to mentor the young women who come into my life, to use my own failures and successes as examples they might be able to learn from. I aim to nurture their confidence, to support their enthusiasm and to remind them that they have the strength, the skills and intelligence to make their vision their reality.

As an expert in branding, I asked Christine, "How can a woman rebrand her life?" She replied, "Know thyself. Understand your core values and the principles that make you tick, that inspire you, fulfill you and that bring you joy. Those values are your own personal 'brand guidelines.'

"From there, do your best to remove from your life the things that do not support your own personal brand standards: negative friends, bad habits, clutter, a job that drains your spirit, hobbies you no longer enjoy (and eat up precious time)—the list goes on and on and will be different for everyone.

"Only you can decide what works for you and what doesn't. Detach from your ego and look at your daily life both subjectively and objectively. You'll see what doesn't fit any longer, you'll see what isn't working to support your vision, what's blurring your vision.

"It isn't always easy to let some things go, but it is absolutely necessary. It will take time and effort, and there will be moments of pain, doubt and grief as you go through the process. Allow yourself to feel those emotions, but don't let them lure you off course or halt your forward momentum. Acknowledge them, take the lessons you can from them and let them go.

"You must do more than just think about your brand: you must live it and embody it. In time, following your personal brand guidelines will become instinctual and organic and you will gain satisfaction, confidence and energy from knowing that in living in accordance with your core values. You will gain the strength, confidence, and enthusiasm to make you the life you desire a reality."

Chapter 4

Manifesting

Trimmed in black tulle rosettes and a smattering of dark sequins, the magnificent black wide-brimmed hat was balanced on my head. With my pinkie sticking out, peering out from under the brim, I delicately sipped my mint tea and wrote.

In my mind, it was real. I imagined that I was a grown woman in charge of my life. However, in reality, I was a gangly awkward fourth-grader. I had thick glasses and cut-off shorts.

I had walked half a mile in dirty sneakers and plunked down some quarters for a cup of tea. In my head, the other customers in a Parisian café were admiring me for my elegance. The truth was, the other customers at the Lou and Hy's Jewish deli in Akron, Ohio were staring, trying to figure out why I had on that huge silly hat!

I felt it so deeply. In that moment, I was transported in my head there.

I am currently writing this chapter from a true French café in Paris. Before I left, my friend and internationally best-selling author Kate Gardner said this about the trip: "Just believe it will happen and it will. With belief, the 'how' shows up." She was correct. The 'how' did show up, and now I have bonded with an incredible group of women authors in Paris.

Angel Tyree:
The Bounce-Back Bitch

Poolside at the amazing historic Roosevelt Hotel in L.A., Hollywood, I interviewed the fabulous Angel Tyree. I met Angel Tyree through our mutual friend, Lucinda Cross, the "Queen of Activation." Angel was her one and only major suggestion for Empowering Women Radio. I had been interviewing a hundred women around the globe, and when Lucinda said, "Angel Tyree," I was like, "I've got to find her," so I was thrilled that I did.

Angel explained the bond that she and Lucinda share: "I had Lucinda Cross on my show a couple of years ago, and she was really an inspiring guest. She had such an amazing, incredible story. More than that, it was a story that sounded like all the girls in the hood where I grew up. It was such a relatable story, and the way in which she overcame the story, overcame her issues. I just loved her.

"I signed off for a couple years and I was not on the air. When I came back to radio, I decided I had to have Lucinda back again. This rekindled our connection. I loved her so much that I brought her out to California to do my very first live conference. She was a keynote on my very first all-day, multi-speaker event, and she totally rocked it, man. Lucinda rocked it."

Angel discussed her own self-discovery process: "My journey started many years ago. I learned a long time ago that if you want to really grow and learn something, you should go to the masters; go to the people who are really kicking ass at it.

"Let me rewind and tell you that when I was young, my dad used to make us listen to, like, Zig Ziglar tapes or Les Brown tapes in the summertime. He would do that and say, 'Pick one off the shelf and give me a report at the end of the summer about it.'

"There would be like twelve cassette tapes, so I was familiar with it. I did it sort of by force as a teenager, but then I sort of stopped for a little bit. But then I just went on this real soul-searching spiritual journey. I just felt like something was burning inside to get to know more about my own spirit and the connection to the Spirit.

"I sought out some of the greats. I went to meet Dr. Wayne Dyer in Maui. I love him. He was so calming to my spirit, but he also communicated in a way that is very digestible and very implementable in your life. He said things that you can really implement and do.

"It's one thing to hear all this airy-fairy stuff that just makes no sense for you, but, like, his things made sense for me, so I applied them to my life. I've gone to see Tony Robbins, Louise Hay, Cheryl Richardson and Brendon

Burchard, Mark Victor Hanson, Jack Canfield... I've gone to see them all. But this is what I've learned.

"Oh and let me tell you, it's not been cheap to see any of them. Their ticket price is no joke, and not only is it pricey, but most of the time, you have to fly to get to them, too. Luckily, some of them are retreats in lovely places like Maui.

"I felt myself worthy enough to invest in, because I think I'm going to be here a long time. I'm hopeful to be here a long time, so if I'm going to do another 50, 60 years around here, then I want to do it the best I possibly can, so I seek out some of the best information.

"I listen to Abraham. I listen to Esther and Gerry Hicks. I'm trying to see Abraham and Esther soon, but they have really fueled my spirit and taught me a lot about the wholeness and the connectedness of us all. And once I really understood that I am not separate from anyone, it changed my view on everything."

Angel explained, "I am still that little girl in the hood that grew up, in a very rough, ghetto neighborhood, as much as I am now this valley girl living in L.A. I'm the same person. I'm all connected. We're all connected.

"It has been a really long quest or self-discovery, and I'm still on it. Every day, I'm meditating or I'm doing EFT tapping. I'm listening to an audio or a meditative CD. I'm still doing that stuff every day.

"I'm still very, very human. I was telling you I still lose my shit about stuff. Things are not always great. I moved across the country (from Florida to L.A.) in a failing relationship. I got pregnant, had a baby, and lost my mom… all in one year.

"I felt like I was on an island by myself. My relationship was not working. I had a baby (and having a baby, in and of itself, can put you on an island). I had lost my mom, and I had no family in town, so I really was deeply feeling I was floating on an island by myself.

"One day, I looked in the mirror. I was having a hard, hard day. I was crying, bawling my eyes out. My face was swollen and wet. My nose was red. It's hard for my nose to get red, because I'm pretty brown. My nose was like Rudolph. I just remember saying like, 'Who is this chick? Who is she?' Because I did not know who I was anymore. I was no longer the mover and shaker that I once was.

"Back in the day, I was always on the scene. I was in all the right places and knew all the right people. At that time, I was in a land where I knew no one. There was a baby on my hip all the time and no part of my career was happening. I was a stay-at-home mom. The situation was controlling me. I felt like it was not me, but I didn't even know who I was anymore.

"I had evolved so much that I was someone different. So I had to discover who that was. I really got back into the things that I had studied before. This time, I dove headfirst into it. You reach a point sometimes in life when it's do or die. When it's make or break.

"…Tony Robbins always says, 'It's either a want or a must.' I got to the point where it was a must. Like, I must figure out who I am now and what is my space here now. I felt like I was floating in and out of every day.

"That's easy to do when you're changing diapers, when you're nursing, when you're on a schedule with a baby. It's easy to float in and out, you know, and that went on for a couple of years. It just wasn't when he was a baby; it was into the toddler years as well.

"I really was like, 'Who am I?' Once I went on that quest of digging, it was a painful truth sometimes and it was a beautiful rediscovery of self. It was a beautiful discovery of self.

"After learning so much, I created the 'Bounce Back to Your Brilliance' tour. We're all born brilliant beings; we just forget it. You know, life hits us. It smacks us. It beats us up. If we're kids, it might spank us. 'Bounce Back to Your Brilliance' is about getting back to that true essence of who we really are. We're brilliant beings. All of us have been knocked off our axis at some point. I talked about one incidence of me being knocked off of mine. There have been many of them. No one has made it past 10 years old and not been knocked off their axis, so it's just about getting back on to your brilliant cycle and keeping it moving.

"'Bounce Back to Your Brilliance' morphed out of a lot of things falling apart in my life, and I thought, 'I've got to bounce back. This state of living is not acceptable.'

"Since then, I started doing a podcast, which has really grown. I'm working on the book based on the bounce-back concept."

Angel explained the "Bounce Back to Your Brilliance" tour: "I went and just flew by the seat of my pants and did an all-day conference at my very first multi-speaker conference. I had 12 speakers in one day. I don't know how I did it.

"Literally, it was just the universe sending people to me, because these are people who get paid to come speak. They don't speak for nothing, and they all showed up for free. Everyone that said, 'Yeah,' I would be like, 'Really? Yes? Really? Are you sure? Okay. Thank you.'

"Even Wendy Gladney-Dean spoke, and she was a keynote. When she came that morning, she said, 'Yeah. All of my friends are like, "Now, who is this person again? How did she get you to show up without paying you?" Wendy said, 'I just don't know. I felt your energy, and it felt like something I wanted to be part of.'

"Your energy sometimes will work for you. Not every time. And I do honestly believe that people should be valued and paid what they're worth for their work and for their information they're sharing. Absolutely, I do. I just wasn't in a space to do it.

"It was my very first event. I was taking a risk on it, anyway, just to do the event. So I just called on 12 speakers, who, I've got to tell you, most of them I found on the Internet. The Internet is amazing. Be careful what you put on the Internet. Be careful, because it can work to your advantage or it can work against you. You never know.

"A lot of people, some of them I had on my podcast before, like Dr. Wayne Purnell, the author of *Choosing Your Power*. I sat next to him at an awards gala. We chatted it up and we had a good time. I ended up having him on my podcast. After being on my podcast, I told him about the event, and like, literally, all I had to do was tell him. He said, 'I'm there.' And I said, 'Well, there's no pay involved.' He repeated, 'I'm there.'

"And he had to fly in, put himself up in a hotel. 'I'm there.' And he was, and he was awesome! He was freaking amazing. There's something that happens when you start making moves and stepping out on faith. I don't like to use all the clichés or all the sayings that people say, but stepping out on faith is really real. If you don't want to call it that, just say 'making a move.'

"You've got to show up for yourself. Show up in your own life. And I just knew it was time for me to show up.

"There were a lot of things transitioning between 2014 and 2015, and I was like, 'I've got to make big moves, and I've got to make big moves now. There's no more waiting for the time to be right, the book to be out, you know, to get my name even bigger... none of that matters right now. I just have to make a move.' And that's what I did.

"I booked a venue. I called on some speakers. Plenty of speakers said, 'No. You're not big enough. Your name is not big enough. You can't pay me. But 12 speakers, 12 really amazing speakers said, 'Yes,' showed up, and rocked it.

"During the big day, at one point, I wasn't really sure how the day was going. I just couldn't gauge it. They seem to be engaged with me. But I was having a hard time determining, 'Is my audience following me? You know, are they having a good time? Are they learning anything?' It was a tough audience to read.

"But at the end of the day, I closed the day out with something that came through me. It downloaded through me and it just shed light on the room. I don't know what it was. I'd have to look at the video to tell you what I said. I have no idea.

"At one point, I was just talking into the microphone, and my eyes were closed, and it's just because I was just receiving and letting it go. When I opened my eyes, all I could see was tears streaming from faces in the first two rows.

"That's when I knew that my work there had been done. I knew that whatever I thought I came to accomplish had been accomplished, and that my work was done. These people did not waste a day in this event. They really showed up for a reason and got something from it.

"At that point, all I could do was bow my head and give blessings and thanks. It was not me... the words just happened to flow through me. I try to allow myself to be a vessel through which the light shines.

"Do not be afraid to sit with the wholeness of who you are. We are complete beings, whole beings. We're not always happy. We're not always overjoyed. We're not always pushing and striving. We're not always on top of our game. Be okay with that sometimes.

"It's the contrast of that that lets us know, and that is so sweet and so good. The brilliance of who we are is the beauty. If we never experience sadness, if we never experience setbacks, if we never experience hard times, then we don't know how good it is when it's good."

Tarra Flores Sloan:
Heart Entrepreneurs Association and Life by My Design

Forward movement is vital in this world to fulfill our purpose. Fabulous California entrepreneur and manifesting mom, Tarra, stated, "For me, manifesting is promoting, changing, or bringing to fruition any burning desire or passion. It has to do with the Law of Attraction and using positive affirmations. Having an optimistic attitude to help manifest your desires can help you to achieve your goals.

"My aspirations are success in business, wealth, health, and happiness. They're all interconnected. Manifesting includes having a vision, creating a plan, and then taking action.

"It is a way to make a positive change. Maybe you're broken-hearted, maybe you have an area in your life that you feel that you deserve better, or you want better. Perhaps you would say, 'I see myself with a new job or a different partner. I imagine more for my kids. I picture a higher level in my career path.'"

I asked Tarra what she has manifested, and she replied, "Whether I have wanted it or not, I believe that I have manifested pretty much everything in my life. And that's hard for some people to swallow because my life has had tragedy and struggle, but it's also been a tremendous blessing for me.

"I can look back to being a young girl and, while I didn't know the term, I was manifesting things into my life. Looking at a dream job description, I have said, 'I lost my job. I don't have anybody to fall back on, but that's the job I want. That's the money I want to make. Let me just go interview for it. What do I need to do to get that job?' And I would just go research. I would spend my last dollar on a really nice, professional résumé and a suit, and I would go and interview for the job I imagined I could do.

"I wasn't always fully qualified, but people took chances on me. They saw my willingness to learn, and knew that I really wanted it. They felt my passion, and I ended up being in places where other people would have to go to school for many years. So, I believe that I've manifested things in my career path.

"My children are very special to me. I believe that I manifested my children, especially my two little ones. There was a time and place when I was in great shape and fit, and then I turned 30, and things kind of just didn't stay the same. I gained some weight and it was really hard to get pregnant. And I went to visit a fertility specialist, and they said, 'Your BMI is a little high. You should try losing weight. That is the number one thing we recommend. Or you can do these other nine things, but they cost a lot of money.'

"I went the route of losing some weight and getting healthy. A month and a half later, I found myself having lost 36 pounds. I also was pregnant shortly thereafter. That was a very special moment in my life. I acknowledge that I manifested that.

"I recently manifested writing and illustrating a series of children's chapter books featuring a 4-year-old girl named Isabella, who goes by Izzy Bella. *Izzy Bella: Not My First Rodeo, My Fourth,* is one of the books. The character is based on my daughter's cute ways.

"If you are starting to manifest things in your life (especially if it is selling a product), I advise that you remain authentic. If you're not authentic, people can tell. They can read it through the words you select. They don't have to see you or know you. They can see that there is an ulterior motive.

"I would say to be authentic, not to copy. Whatever you're really passionate about, that is going to reach and help someone. The ultimate goal is to help other people. If you have something to offer someone, that person will be attracted to you and maybe buy something that you happen to have for sale.

"I think a woman can be empowered at any age. It can happen at any time. It has to do with awareness and their consciousness.

"When you are empowered, there is a release of judgment from yourself or from other women. You let go of the worries such as thinking, 'Well, she has that and I don't,' or 'I haven't made it yet.'

"You don't have yesterday. Tomorrow is not here yet. You just have right now, and you are living so powerfully in this particular moment that all of your power rests in that moment. That's an empowered woman."

Tarra explained the odds that she overcame to find prosperity and happiness: "Very young parents raised me. My mom was 16, and my dad was just a little older, and he was an immigrant. And they were not prepared to have children at such a young age.

"I wasn't expected to finish high school when I was younger, or to get a job, or finish college, and I did all of that. We lived in a beautiful home, but inside, behind the walls of that, was dysfunction and abuse. I was around guns and drugs and violence. You name it... I've been there. And where I am today, it's tremendous: beauty, stability, and freedom.

"Fortunately, I've had women come into my life and mentor me. They haven me under their wing throughout the years, and especially recently, in this last five or six years, I've had especially beautiful women mentor me. I think some women are like, 'Gosh, I wish I had that.'

"A lot of times, you'll see men blessed with their built-in system of acceptance and respect, acknowledgment, and friendship. It's like a timeless, mutual agreement of their co-existence in their social settings, their endeavors or aspirations. It translates into whatever financial worth or lack of what they choose to create, like all is possible for men.

"But for women, obviously, all is also possible. Unfortunately, women don't always believe this. So our time with mutual agreement has been an innate competition. You know, you size a woman up. It's her appearance, intelligence, success, and wealth. It's judgment, and I found that that's all wrong.

"I've had more success, wealth, and personal growth— spiritually and business-wise—by helping other women succeed in whatever passion they have. And it turns out that their success is my own success, and I have learned that through my mentors.

"I see that my mentors love standing up to clap and cry out of elation for my success. I'm seeing that from personal experience. And when I do that for other women, it's our success. It feels like, 'Oh, my. I found my life's purpose,' you know.

"My mentor, Dani NirMcGrath, is a perfect example. Dani has really blossomed in her career. She set and reached a high fitness goal, and her yoga practice is excellent. She really commands herself in a very unique and special way. Everything she touches is gold, from friendships to business.

"While I want you to see where I am now with my businesses, books, and family, I feel you should know that I have come from struggle. I am a survivor. I haven't always had the best family environment. I was not given the tools to succeed; I had to seek them out even when I didn't know they were there for me to find.

"When I found what my 'why' is, that changed everything for me. So for me, my 'why's are my daughters (Maureen and Isabella) and my son (Adrian) and my husband. They are the reason why I do everything.

"But there was a time, for ten years, when I was a single mom. I had come from an experience that was dysfunctional. I went through my life as a single mom, rising through the ranks in the corporate world. I fought discrimination because I was a young, single mom.

"I finally just ignored all that. I filled in the blank of 'I am.' I said that to myself over and over and over. 'I am,' and I filled in the blank. 'I am,' and I filled in the blank. Even if I wasn't there yet, I still kept saying that. I would add what I wanted to be, what I wanted to become, where I wanted to go, what I wanted to have, and that I deserved it all.

"I am someone who deserves every success. Everything that has happened to me is just a stepping-stone for tomorrow and the next day and the next day.

"I attracted a circle full of people who lift me up in life. My mantra is, 'My life, by my design. Live now.' There is a power within you and me. It wells up. It's a reminder saying, 'You're amazing. You can do anything.' It's absolutely true. I'm living proof of that.

"I do what I'm passionate about, and that always precedes financial wealth for me. Working from home while being a mom: that is my passion. My greatest joy is my babies. Whatever your 'why' is, that's what you should focus on in life. You should do everything in your power to follow your passion so that you can live for your 'why'!"

Chapter 5:

Vibrations

Everyone's energy has a certain vibration. When you are attuned to it, you can sense it when you strike up a conversation with a person. There are visual clues such as body language and tone of voice that can be identified as either positive or negative energy.

When I go on business and keynoting trips with my assistant, we watch to be sure that our vibrations are high. When this occurs, amazing connections are formed with other people and, as if by magic, things start to fall into place.

When the vibrations are low, we face negative experiences in a domino effect and tend to attract other miserable people into our lives. Brittany Comer, who helped me on this project, has served as my "Vibrational Accountability Partner." When I would get low, she would help me recognize that, and vice versa, so that we could get back on course.

Caryn Chow:
America's "Love Your Life" Coach

Brittany (my assistant during a part of the Common Threads project) grew so much during our time together. I recall the moment that her life started to click and an understanding washed over her. It was in the hotel room in N.Y.C. when I interviewed Caryn Chow. Brittany sat in the room wide-eyed, soaking up the information on vibrations and manifesting. Brittany gained so much during our adventures that she decided to follow her dream to move across the country to L.A.

Caryn Chow is America's "Love Your Life" coach, and I could immediately see why. Her energy is contagious and her smile lights up a room. The second time I interviewed Caryn, she was in her home and was able to verbally walk the listeners through her house so that we could understand the setting. How one lives is important in understanding who one is.

Caryn explained her chameleon-like presence that can be felt when she is on stage or just one-on-one coaching: "I can morph. I am skilled at matching my personality to yours. I can blend. I can change your mood if you're going through something. But I will not, and choose not to, tolerate bad energy. Instead, I will raise my vibrations to envelope yours with love."

She believes that it is important to create space that we live and work in that has positive vibes. Caryn describes her living environment: "My haven is clear of clutter. It's got a Zen feeling, and that changes my energy instantaneously. When I come from the subway, off the streets of New York and into my home, my energy shifts. It is because of what I surround myself with in my home. It is about the lighting, the mood, and the energy. It's all connected.

"I practice meditation every day, so I'm looking at this beautiful, foot-long, silver Buddha, and it's just putting a smile on my face. I'm breathing as I look at it. It reminds me to breathe, and breathing is part of energy.

"The mirrors in my home are literally a reflection of how I'm feeling. When I look in the mirror and I see myself looking a little bit sad or whatever, it reminds me that things aren't that bad. I try to alter my mood by starting with my face. Smiling instantly changes your mood. People don't give enough credit to smiling.

"Smiling goes a long way to change how you feel, but also it changes how others feel. You walk into a store and someone has had a bad day, a little smile goes a long way, and I know you've done this, Dr. Shellie. I know a lot of other people have, too. It's just lifting another person instantly lifts you as well.

"So all these things in my home, from the Buddha statue to the lighting and mirrors—and even my little Christmas tree—they are all part of filling my energy with positivity."

I, of course, asked Caryn Chow to discuss manifesting. She lit up and said, "Oh my goodness, 'manifesting' has become my favorite word in the dictionary. First of all, to manifest, you should remove certain words from your dictionary. Those include 'can't' or 'maybe' or 'try.' Those words don't exist in my vocabulary anymore. You just move forward.

"To manifest, you have to start with what you feel first. It's about vibrating to manifest. You have to have that inner vibration that comes with enlightenment, and there are ways to get there. So it's not like just saying, 'Okay, I'm going to manifest this today.' That is part of it.

"The visualization portion of it is very important, but it's not just about that, because anybody can do that. You have to go inside. And when you do that inner work and you start to vibrate that, it starts to vibrate outside of your body from the inner to the outer, and there's work that needs to be done. Once it starts to happen, you start to manifest on a daily basis."

Caryn described how this fits into being a communicator: "The way I like to explain it is, when you're out there speaking to the world on a public forum or you're speaking one-on-one to a client or to a loved one, communicating is vital. It's not just about words. It's about how to express yourself.

"How you talk to yourself is of the utmost importance. It's about negative self-talk. You hear a lot about that these days, right? It's about exchanging good habits in lieu of bad, and it all starts from your mindset.

"There is a great deal of emphasis today on mindfulness. You can't be mindful if you don't have the right mindset. Everything starts from within. People don't realize that. It is not just taking the practical steps. You have to go in reverse first. And I'm not saying go back way to your past. I'm saying sometimes you have to take three steps back to take a leap forward, and that's the beginning of manifestation and vibration, going back inside."

I know that some of my listeners and readers may not understand the concept, and so I asked Caryn to elaborate. "Vibration is nothing more than energy. So what energy are you putting out? What energy is the other person receiving from you?

"Picture a stage. You get on it to perform. If you are in a bad mood to begin with, unless you have the technique where you can just snap your finger and turn it on like, 'The show must go on.' You might go on stage and bring your entire negative mood with you. The bad mood could come from just breaking up with your boyfriend, or someone just screamed at you out on the street, or something is going on inside, and you bring it there to the stage. You are going to manifest that on stage because it's coming from outside of you. You are vibrating your energy and projecting it to the people who are watching you.

"That's all vibration is: it's energy. You have to work on the energy that you're feeling. Harness the power to do great things."

Melanie LaPatin:
Dancing with the Stars and
So You Think You Can Dance

In NYC, I sat down with world champion Melanie LaPatin, the choreographer for So You Think You Can Dance and Dancing with the Stars. She has trained Pierce Brosnan, Renee Russo, Tim Robbins, Robin Williams, Vanessa Williams, Patrick Stewart, and more. We met through Andrew Pueschel, one of my favorite doctoral students who taught me the choreography for the stage to perform "All That Jazz" from the musical Chicago.

I had a blast getting to know Melanie and learning about her dance. She teaches salsa, tango, cha-cha, and all the ballroom dances. Melanie works with a range from beginners to world champions.

Melanie has so much insight about the celebrities and their dance abilities. In fact, she told me that Barbara

Walters can dance and that her dad ran a famous nightclub way back called the Latin Quarter.

For Entertainment Weekly, she has done the breakdowns of what the days are like working on the television show So You Think You Can Dance. Melanie explained that the biggest obstacle is, "Teaching a non-ballroom dancer how to be fabulous in five hours. It is not just the choreography; it is actually teaching the technique. The amount of turns, the partnering, and the connection between the couple can't be faked. The judges are looking, and what makes it look smooth and makes it look magical is the technique. We don't have time to set that up. It takes years to get technique. Baryshnikov spent every day doing his basics. It is the same thing with ballroom dancers, and we have five hours to take non-ballroom dancers and get them there. Fortunately, the kids are extremely talented or they wouldn't be in the top twelve on the TV show."

I asked how they were able to achieve professional-looking dance pieces with amateurs. Melanie explained, "We say as much as possible in a very small amount of time. As much information as we can give them.

"Great ones want the information so badly that they won't let us sit down when we are done. They continue to ask more questions. The more they ask, the more we want to give. It is wonderful for us that these kids want this information and they love it. They end up loving it even if they have never done it before. Just like when I was on Dancing with the Stars with the celebrities.

"I have the heart of a teacher. It is so empowering when a student gets it, when the light bulb goes off. They feel the passion. They are living it. I can give them what is joyful to me, and they get it.

"I am also a natural connector. I love to hook people up with other people. I have no problems in any social settings. Like we are right now having a wonderful connection. It is like it's just the two of us and there is no one else in the world. Having a real connection feels wonderful. I make them easily because of my career.

"I like to introduce the average person to dance. I am such a promoter because it changes people's lives at any age. People say to me, 'I have always wanted to ballroom dance.' I say, 'Here is my number. I will hook you up with a studio with a teacher anywhere in the world that you are.' I give that to them. The gift of connection is a wonderful thing to be able to give. Then I see people at a conference and they say, 'Oh my gosh! You gave me that number. It changed my life. I love it. I am so happy!'

"I put myself out there because I love to share dance with people, not just as the typical ballroom dancer. I have gone to many fundraisers donating lessons, and I do a lot of Broadway events. Tony (my dance partner) and I used to go to the authentic Latin clubs and the real swing clubs. We took Pasa Doble lessons in the early 80's from flamingo dancers when no one else in the ballroom world was doing that. We brought the authenticity on the ballroom dance world.

"To excel in your chosen field, start by working on your core beliefs. We can say we want something, but we need to really believe it. We need to be able to visualize it."

We talked about Melanie's artistic thought process. She stated, "My brain is everywhere, constantly. I have to say to myself, 'Okay, stop. Melanie, be quiet. Be still.' I am always coming up with creative ideas.

"As I was waiting for you in the lobby before we taped the show, I had this idea that I had to write down. I guarantee you this little electronic device will be coming out shortly that I dreamed up in my head. Tony will send me a text and he will be like, 'Okay, here is another one of your ideas,' and he will send me a picture of that thing I said was going to be invented. It's like it has been manifested."

Melanie explained, "To manifest something is to make something come to pass. I didn't think I did that very often, yet I have done it quite a bit. I have allowed myself.

"I manifested being well-known from my TV appearances. You know how Caryn Chow was in this room, interviewing before me? She squealed, 'Melanie LaPatin!' when I opened the door and she saw me.

"I am always pleasantly surprised when people know who I am. I get it in the street all the time. It is nice for a moment. You think, 'Oh, that's cool,' and then it is on to the next right step, whatever that might be.

I inquired about other things that Melanie feels she has manifested over the years. She said, "I manifested a fabulous dance studio in Times Square. Tony and I have manifested over 100 world championship titles. We manifested being World Cabaret champions. I loved that piece. It was a bluesy, Aretha Franklin piece of music with lifts. I said to Tony, 'We have got to do something with this.' We did it to 'Dr. Feelgood' by Aretha Franklin. We entered it into a world championship cabaret and we won. And it's a good feeling to win.

"Ladies, someday you will discover (if you haven't already) where your heart is and what you believe is your reason for being on this earth to do. I believe we are here to constantly create and recreate ourselves. This can continue until we are doing what we are supposed to do. Once we are there... give it away. Share your gifts and information with whomever might need it. Do it with love."

Chapter 6:

Mentoring

When you create a mentoring relationship with a woman whom you admire, the learning opportunities can be immense. I will never forget the process of writing my fourth book, *Mentoring Magic: Pick the Card for Your Success*. Claudia was a doctoral student of mine who approached me after my lecture on "Query to Print in a Publish-or-Perish World."

Claudia was working for a Fortune 500 company on their internal mentoring program. She explained to me that she felt she had a book inside of her that would help to find, form, and sustain mentoring relationships. After she graduated with her Ph.D., we sat down for coffee and began the process of my mentoring her through the book-writing process.

This morphed from a mentoring relationship to a co-author colleague relationship because it was so reciprocal. I deeply value my relationship with my mentee, Dr. Claudia Armani Bavaro.

That is important to note. In a good mentoring relationship, both parties receive something from it.

Eva Sztupka-Kerschbaumer:
EsSpa Kozmetika Skin Care

I instantly felt my body start to relax and I let out a sigh of relief as I entered the EsSpa. The soothing music and scents of lavender wafted through the air. I could immediately see why people love to get facials from Eva Sztupka-Kerschbaumer.

Eva Sztupka-Kerschbaumer is the owner of EsSpa. Eva believes strongly in mentoring, and she counted on the guidance of her lady customers at the spa when she first moved to the States from Hungary. She recalled, "It definitely was women who first helped me. Clients were like, 'Oh, you need to get an attorney; tell your husband.'

"Women who would tell me names of attorneys or who to go to and tell him this, tell him that—I appreciate it to this day. Even when I had my first car, the client saw me walking out with laundry bags. She said, 'Why are you…?' I said, 'I don't have a washer and dryer.' She said, 'I'm going to write you a check. I can do this, just get a washer and dryer in here. I don't want to see you dragging laundry. I want to see you doing amazing facials.'"

When I first asked her what 'empowerment' was to her, she focused on the word 'power.' Eva stated, "Power, to me, as a little young student, made me think of Lenin's and Stalin's picture. Power was authority. Power was bad or controlling people or things. You're controlling your history; your teachers were telling you different than what really happened, because they were controlled. So that's what power meant to me."

Eva and I talked about the difference between the terminology of 'power' versus 'empowering.' We also considered that since she is from Hungary, her association of the words 'respect' and 'power' are with "somebody you're scared of, and that's why you respect them." She wondered out loud, "Or does this mean that you acknowledge something they do as good? It's also an interesting word coming from a socialist or communist country."

After we talked, she realized that she feels empowered when she puts her foot down and declares to her husband, "Absolutely not. This is the way I want something." Then she tells him, "There's nothing you can do about it." She explains that when she takes the leadership role at work and declares that something should be done her way, she feels empowered.

She went on to explain, "The second part of this empowerment, I feel from my staff. I feel like they are my ultimate supporters. So, I've started feeling that my staff really looks up to what I have to say.

"I have had to make hard decisions knowing that they would not like it. But I have a way of making them comfortable by saying, 'Wait, I've been there. I was an employee before. I know what has to happen for the business. This is just the best decision right now. If something else comes up, if I made a mistake, I will take responsibility.'

"I think that empowerment is you taking responsibility for your actions. That's how I feel. If you made a bad business choice, you might have to say to yourself, 'Okay, this was not a smart thing. I will have to pick up myself and I will fix it.' I'm a fixer. I always like to fix things, even in the bathroom. If the toilet gets plugged, I'm always there with a plunger somewhere. I'm fixing things."

Eva talked about how she gets things accomplished: "You have to know exactly what you want and you have to visualize yourself doing it. Make connections with people in that field and seek out help. Just ask them. What is the worst they can say? 'I can't help you.' I'm going to tell you right now that this is not going to happen. They will guide you!

"I loved when I found out that somebody was doing power walks, 'Walking with Mentors.' I think it was in Central Park in New York. Oprah would walk with a total stranger, a woman, and give her advice. I think we should do that. Just do these walks where we could give ideas and share, because I'm sure that she would need an idea about something, and I would love to hear her strategies and suggestions."

I looked into the 'Walking with Mentors' program that Eva described while researching at the Schlesinger Library on the history of women in America at Harvard University. I discovered while reading *Stiletto Networks* how the mentor walks began with powerhouse Geraldine Laybourne, who grew the television network for children, Nickelodeon, into an $8 million enterprise. Laybourne had become known for her hard work behind the scenes and her cocktail-infused power meetings with small groups of ladies over a 16-year-period.

As Pamela Ryckman in *Stiletto Network: Inside the Women's Power Circles That Are Changing the Face of Business* explained, "As her reputation spread, people sought her out, but Laybourne couldn't meet with everyone and still do her job. So her assistant started scheduling walks with 'mentees' around Central Park at 7 a.m. Sometimes she'd stroll the loop and end up with a cup of coffee, and other times she'd amble in the Bramble. During the years that she lived on Central Park West at 64th street, Layborne walked with more than 100 aspirants."

The concept morphed into "mentor walks" in 2005. Four hundred women, including stars like Meryl Streep, Marlo Thomas, and Diane von Furstenberg, participated. These spread to Oxygen's "Mentor Walks" in 10 cities.

I was so glad that Eva mentioned this walking way of mentoring. I feel it would be an awesome component for the future of the Global Sisterhood of Empowering Women! Even if, informally, ladies around the world would find mentors and start walking and talking together, it could be a very powerful movement internationally.

Uraidah Hassani:

The Women Worldwide Initiative

Uraidah Hassani is a colleague who I met with at Senator Kristen Gillibrand's Woman's Economic Empowerment Summit at NYU. Uraidah explained her organization: "The Women's Worldwide Initiative's mission is really to connect, inspire, and educate women and girls on a global scale. We do this through community-based mentorship programs and small-scale international development projects that aim to strengthen women and girls' capacity as decision-makers.

"Therefore, our programs are dedicated to youth development, to social and economic empowerment, and, generally, women and girls in underserved communities in New York City, as well as in developing countries. At the heart of it, our work really focuses on elevating girls' and women's voices and empowering their position in the world."

Uraidah explained her heritage: "I am half-Dutch and half-Persian. I'm also a Muslim. With hindsight, I see how growing up, I really struggled with my own identity. I wondered if I was good enough and where I belonged or fit into my immediate community, which was hard because my community changed often.

"When I lived in Texas, with my brown, curly hair, all the kids usually just assumed (due to pigeon-holing) that I was Mexican. As a kid, you don't want to be different, so I kind of felt, 'Well, whatever.' Unfortunately, that meant I was prolonging diving into my own self and discovering what my Persian and/or Dutch heritage means to me?

"Then we were also moving around to all these urban communities like London, Chicago, and New York. I think those were the areas that I was able to really find myself in that diversity.

"Coming into your own and finding your identity can be tricky. I came from a mixed-race immigrant background. Also, being a woman of color who did move around a lot as a child, I had to blend into these different communities wherever I went. I believe that really played a role in both my desire to start this organization and also for our programs to target women and girls who are in marginalized or in underserved communities."

She described what it is like to live as a Muslim in America: "It's been an ordeal that's included being interrogated at the airport at the age of 12 for four hours.

Also, I was ostracized for my background and my religion on numerous occasions.

"I feel that this distinct form of feeling like an outsider; the community doesn't want you to be a part of it. But it's also allowed me to gain a lens into how other marginalized communities facing discrimination in the U.S. feel. I understand the outsider feeling that the girls that I work with in East New York and Brownsville in Brooklyn feel with the rest of society.

"I have experienced feeling unwelcome in certain circles or certain events. I think that my passion to really provide a safe place for women and girls to find their voice and identity stems from wanting to help them discover their potential. Out of these experiences and sometimes feeling unwelcome in certain circles or certain events came my passion to really provide a safe place for women and girls to find their voice and identity."

We talked about being a feminist in today's America. Uraidah explained, "There is not much inequality left. It's here, though. And knowing that one in every three women is likely to be beaten, coerced into sex, or otherwise abused at least once in her lifetime anywhere in the world can shed light on this fact. Women do two-thirds of the world's work, receive 10% of the world's income, and they own 1% of the means of production. One woman dies in childbirth every minute. Women face unfairness that can be hard to fathom sometimes, especially in other areas of the world as well."

We talked about specific initiatives that her organizations are implementing in America and abroad.

Dr. Jeanine Blackburn:
Kolor 'N Kiln and the National Black
MBA Association

Dr. Jeanine Blackburn is the president of the National Black MBA Association. She is an entrepreneur who started the Kolor 'N Kiln studio after training trainers in a Fortune 500 company for decades. My children and I love to go to her new studio to paint and create works of art together. Jeanine Blackburn was one of my doctoral students, and we actually have a joint U.S. patent for a training program we created together called Differentiated Design™.

Dr. Jeanine Blackburn described the Black MBA Association: "The organization is about economic empowerment for people who have their MBA degrees and who happen to be of African-American descent. What we do is pull all of these highly-intelligent individuals together, find opportunities in the job market, and conduct personal development.

"There are 45 different chapters throughout the United States, but we're all headquartered out of Chicago. It's a great organization to be part of because it's about giving back on so many different levels. The work we do around education starts with high school students from 8th grade up through the graduate program. We're able to give back college scholarships. Last year, we gave away close to $300,000 in college scholarship money. Being a mentor helping out with these kids in 8th grade to see that there's a bigger world than just what's in their community, that's really exciting."

We worked very closely as I advised her dissertation. Dr. Jeanine Blackburn spoke about her topic as she obtained her Ph.D.: "My dissertation topic focused on understanding how people learn in a corporate environment. In that environment, you are not evaluated how you learn. So many individuals come into a company, and if they're taught not according to how they learn, they could be passed over, or, eventually, they could even be asked to leave the company since they don't learn the needed information. But it could be that it is just not presented in the way that they learn.

"I determined, based on my research, that if companies take the time to evaluate how individuals learn and modify to that learning style by differentiating the learning to how the majority of their employees learn, the productivity will go up, the retention of the information that is being presented will improve and taught will be retained. When I go out and I speak to other companies, it's exciting to tell them about the research that I did and how I have proof that it works."

Dr. Blackburn and I discussed the importance of women finding those connections and sustaining relationships with each other. She and I started off in a professor/student relationship that morphed into a dear friendship.

Dr. Blackburn recalled, "In the beginning, Shellie, you and I started off as the professor and the student. Over three years, we connected as friends. We found that we had a lot of things in common, but more importantly, we were passionate about so many of the same topics. It is really great for women all over to come together, to be able to share their stories, or find a way to mentor each other.

"A lot of times, we don't even take the time to do that. We're so busy focused on our families and our careers; we really don't think about how we can mentor each other. As you and I found, there were times that I could be the teacher and you could be the student. It is important for us, as women, just to stay connected and say, 'Hey, you know what? We're strong individuals. We can really help each other out.'"

Dr. Jeanine Blackburn and I discussed Empowering Women Radio and *Common Threads* connecting women literally all over the globe. Dr. Blackburn said, "I think this is a great platform for you. Knowing you as my dissertation coach and my friend, I can see why you have done this work. You have been a visionary. This is something you talked about three years ago, and seeing this come to fruition, it makes me excited.

"In my travels, when I'm able to connect with women outside of my community, I see that we have a lot of things in common, but we did not have a platform where we can share that commonality. Now we have that platform, so I'm just excited.

"Listening to the other women who you interviewed, I thought, 'It is awesome to see this come to light.' I could feel that women all over the world will be able to stay connected. How empowering is that?

"What I would like to share with ladies internationally is to get to know yourself. Take that moment to determine your strength and what you have to offer. A lot of times, we are so focused on taking care of family, our sisters, and worrying about our job, but when you take a moment to dig deep, you can get to know who you are and even start journaling things about yourself.

"Talk to yourself as if you're talking to a friend. What do you love about yourself? And when you start to journal that information, you will start to see how successful you are and you're talking your own story. We all hear stories about other women, about how successful they have become, but what is your story?

"I took a moment and started journaling why I felt successful. I am determined. I'm able to share that story and I feel that every women needs to take the time to do that. Take your story and share it; keep connecting with other people throughout the world. And that's why I'm so passionate about the platform that Dr. Shellie has going on, and I can feel myself getting emotional about it. I am so proud of you. When I see all these things that you're doing, it's just another way to keep me inspired and keep me motivated. I'm glad to tell people, 'Hey, that's my friend.

Not only is Dr. Shellie Hipsky an amazing professor, but she wears so many different hats.' And your story is something that we all can take a lesson from. We can find a little piece of ourselves in that thread."

Haseena Patel:

Leave No Girl Behind International

With today's technology, mentorship and teaching can happen from anywhere. Mentoring can occur with women young and old, wherever they are. Haseena and Shameema Patel are sisters who run the Leave No Girl Behind International movement based in South Africa.

Haseena shared the experience of leading power circles via Skype from the U.S. with South African high school girls. "When we started our first girls' power circles and were preparing for the Empowered Girl/Empowered World 2013 conference, we got the sponsorships in place and we really wanted the girls to participate because it was being held at the schools in St. Dominic's Academy. We got other schools to participate as well. The girls in the school we worked with needed to participate, and they had the opportunity to shine.

"Shameema and I asked them, 'Who wants to be involved? Is there anyone who's interested?' They just like looked at each other and no one said they were interested. So I told them the story about how I wished that when I was in school that someone had not just focused on my academics (because I was really smart), but had also stretched me in other areas and challenged me. I urged them to, 'Do something new. It will be critical for you.' So they partnered up and we gave them topics for an impromptu speech, and we chose for them.

"As time went on, when we asked for volunteers for something, the volunteers came forward because they felt secure. They felt that they weren't going to be judged. Or at least they wouldn't be laughed at by each other. We also take a pledge at the beginning so that they know whatever they say in the group stays confidential.

"Haseena and I talked about my Skype lessons in South Africa: "It's a gathering of girls, aged between 12 to 18 years, who want to make a difference in their communities. They have a safe, secure environment. It's supervised by Leave No Girl Behind International's power circle.'

"During our first power circle, Shellie and I were both together with a facilitating teacher, Janie. They get together weekly and they learn to empower themselves and others and share, so they're able to learn and teach. They take part in various community projects, learning to serve as well.

"They are able to develop into power circle mentors should they want to start leading their own power circles. It is certainly a place for them to be themselves, to be accepted for who they are, and we actually see that there's a lot of growth with the girls. You don't necessarily see it from week-to-week, but when we were preparing for Empowered Woman/Empowered World 2013, we witnessed the difference.

"Our goal is to build girls' power circles in every possible country. We need to train power circle mentors. In the future we will empower power circle groups and have ambassadors in every country to coordinate the power circles.

"The girls Skype with amazing women like you, Dr. Shellie. You have so much to share with them because you're such an empowered woman, who is successful in so many areas of life, and you've got a wonderful story. You made such a difference in their lives. Now they can see what is out there and what's possible for them. The girls in South Africa, they felt so special having you broadcast all the way from Pennsylvania, U.S.A."

Haseena discussed her mentors and women she looked up to with Empowering Women Radio: "I was taught in a Catholic school run by Dominican nuns. They were role models for me because if something needed to be done, they went forward in their faith and their strength. They were doing what needed to be done through their example. I think that really empowered me.

"I had a music teacher, I remember her, and she was in her 80's when I was about 10 or 11, and she was bent over and had white hair, but I never saw her as old because she was always in control. She was confident and empowered."

I asked Haseena how she defined an empowered woman. She replied, "She needs to be independent, to believe in herself, and to know that she doesn't need a man by her side. There's nothing wrong with a man by her side—men are great—but she doesn't need it.

"I think more than that, an empowered woman is someone who has the tools and has the belief in herself. She can find her purpose and her calling in this world and to effect positive change."

Haseena discussed the obstacles she encountered in her life: "For me, there was a bit of a generational and cultural gap, because while I'm Indian and South African, my parents were also. My dad was born in India, but when he was 10, he came to South Africa. And my mom was born in South Africa. However, those remnants of culture are kind of still there. I was not really into that culture at all, so I guess I was the one that kind of clashed.

"When I was a girl, everyone looked at their parents and they kind of had the same lifestyle as their parents. They understood their problems. Their parents could say things like, 'I was dating this guy and this happened and I understand how you feel.' Well, I never had that, so I always had to look to myself to make my own rules; there was no sort of role or no place that I fitted into. I was always the square peg being hammered into the wrong hole by everyone.

"It was destructive for me because it led to me not believing in myself. It really took many years for me to get through that and discover myself. I know exactly who I am today, but maybe I wouldn't if I didn't have those obstacles to deal with."

When she was asked why we continue to strive for gender equality, Haseena stated, "The question 'why' is very important. My talk at the Empowered Girl/Empowered World was on 'The Power of Why.' Just the fact that we're asking that great question is important because you're asking me so that you can see my point of view. However, a lot people ask that same question because they don't see any reason for it. And that's the problem that we have. If you have to ask why, then there already is a reason for it.

"If we look in, for example, the Middle Eastern countries, some of the African countries, rural Africa, you can see that there's a long way to go, because if you're born female, you're born with a huge disadvantage in the sense that you're not valued as much as your male counterparts are.

"Also, just for both of us who are born in free countries—for instance, the U.S.A. is basically the freest country there is, yet there is a need for gender equality because there's still the difference in value. So that's what we're working towards.

"We do that in many ways. With the Empowered Girl/Empowered World annual conference, we would like to see that in more countries. Perhaps Shellie and I can Skype in or even go in person as guest speakers. We would like to see in every country power circles for girls.

"At the moment, we have our South African ambassadors for Leave No Girl Behind. A conference attendee is taking this to China. Obviously, we want girls in the U.S. to have power circles. We would especially love to see them in countries around the world where there is blatant discrimination against women."

We spoke about how Leave No Girl Behind International began. "We were busy writing a book called *Leave No Girl Behind* and getting the input of women around the world. That book evolved to include a vision about how can we change the world. We began to look at the bigger picture of what a girl becoming empowered actually does.

"Every girl who grows up and decides to have a family, if that girl was educated, it will influence the family. She has the power to influence generations to come, and that's what Leave No Girl Behind International is based upon.

"We have various programs to educate girls, to empower them. Some that can be used in third-world countries, some that can be used anywhere around the world. Empower every girl, everywhere, because even if she's living in the lap of luxury, that does not mean that she's automatically empowered.

"Our first mission is to empower girls directly. To raise awareness about how girls' empowerment can effect change in this world, to get the world involved. Let them know how we can actually change the generation and generations to come. An empowered girl means an empowered nation, which means an empowered generation."

Chapter 7:

Abundance

I have been wealthy, poor, and most levels in-between. I know what it feels like to dig around on the floor of a beat-up minivan searching for change in the cracks of the seats... to get gas so I can pick up my baby from daycare. I am now living a life that I had only dreamed of a few years ago, complete with true financial stability. "Abundance" is equal to success and wealth in many circles.

Stephanie Nickolich:
Style Your Success

Stephanie Nickolich is the founder of the Success Society. She is making some major waves with women around the globe who are looking for their own personal success. She chatted with Empowering Women Radio about her organization, which recently conducted the first Collabo-Rich conference online.

Stephanie said that the Success Society is, "Growing very rapidly, which is awesome. Success Society, which women can join at StyleYourSuccess.com, was founded out of my own personal need for affordable resources and tools when I was growing my first business, Accessory Fanatic.

"The first year of my business, I was struggling significantly. I lacked the community piece. I felt very alone, and I didn't think that anyone could possibly relate to this emotional roller coaster ride that I felt that I was on. And the truth is, when you're starting running and growing a business, those emotional, crazy feelings are pretty normal. I was just overwhelmed, overworked, significantly underpaid, and I was trying to figure out a way to keep all the pieces together.

"So, really, when I was creating Success Society, it was truly a reflection of what I was able to go through in my own personal journey. Also, I recognized the need for affordable resources and tools to help women create lives and businesses that they love.

"I've been really blessed. We're growing organically, but we have several ways in which we work with women. Our platform is entirely free and open to all women to jump on and join us. I encourage every woman out there to go ahead and do that.

"The first way is through educational content. We have great blog articles that can help women build brands, build businesses, and balance their lives while running, growing, and starting a company. Or if they're still corporately employed, we teach them how to run a successful side hustle. We have great contributors with a bunch of success stories, shared by women that have been able to overcome obstacles in their journey and accomplish success on so many levels.

"We also have a sophisticated board of C.E.O.s that are experts in our industry, and they teach new online content in the form of e-courses monthly that our paid members have access to. So we have affordable mentoring and education.

"One of the most significant pieces in my journey, is having a mentor in building a business was the built-in accountability. So we've actually customized accountability tools for our members to use. It tracks their goals, their progress, and it rewards them based on creating positive changes."

Stephanie talked with me about an obstacle that she had in her personal success. Stephanie said, "After the first year of my business, when I still owned Accessory Fanatic—we're in transition (actually, we are selling our name)—I was burnt out and really frustrated. I felt like everything was difficult. Now life and business are not difficult anymore.

"I had to get really clear on what the bigger picture was for me and what I wanted to achieve—not only for myself, but also for my family and women worldwide. And I had to get clear with what am I most passionate about. The truth is that there were pieces of my passion raveled throughout Accessory Fanatic, but it wasn't everything that I truly believed in.

"Success Society is a reflection of that from all different angles. My greatest values, beliefs, loves, and passions are still greatly intertwined into what we do there.

"I think I had to get really clear on what I wanted, and I had to let the world know. At first, I used to hide behind the brand that I created. It was time that I really put myself out to the world. And when people got to know who I really am, it not only helped me, but it helped my business, too.

"The other thing is I invested in myself. I got a mentor. I still work with him today, and I was seeking out the guidance and support from somebody who has the mindset and the money game that I wanted who believed in my mission and vision just as much as I did. Due to his mentoring, I was able to get out of my own way.

"A coach or mentor isn't only there to bounce ideas off of; rather, they truly hold you accountable. I mean, I was very uncomfortable at moments in this journey, before it got more comfortable.

"I was digging up things that I didn't even realize were keeping me stuck. There were stories that I was telling myself that were prohibiting my success. Speaking with an expert truly pulled that out of me. I could see why I am feeling this way. Where my energy is going right now. The truth is that I was living in fear because I couldn't see the future, because I couldn't see two feet in front of my current situation.

"I don't have a problem with that anymore, because I was able to face it and I was able to work with it. We put tools and techniques in place in my life and my business that helped me through that. There was hand-holding. There was butt-kicking, when necessary. But I think for me, the most significant piece was that I was accountable. I showed up. I did the work required, and I didn't make excuses. I took ownership.

"I really, really, really wanted it, and I think that's so important in working with a mentor. Because there is no magic pill that you can take in life or business that's going to change your life or circumstances. The only one that can truly make the changes is yourself. The guidance and the support and accountability are also absolutely key in accomplishing success.

"I work with a lot of women on a daily basis, and I actually see the same self-limiting beliefs coming up over and over again. I think women, especially, are very different when we do business than men. We're much more emotional creatures, and we actually can be our own biggest critics. There are several things that go into that, and one is perfection paralysis. We are not able to put something out for the world because the fear of being judged, it not being good enough, or we're not experienced; whatever. Whatever the 'enough' is.

"The thing is, we have all the tools that it takes within ourselves to become successful—to run, grow, and create successful businesses and lives. But it does take getting out of our own way and first identifying what actually those beliefs are that are keeping us stuck.

"Women, we go through life and we accumulate all of this mental clutter, and it can stem all the way back to when we were children. Maybe we were bullied when we were in school, and now this has created this life-long belief that we've been carrying around that we're not good enough.

"My mentor was able to gauge my energy and see these fears that I was having in business that were prohibiting me from achieving success. My fears were coming from something that was rooted somewhere deeper in my life. Maybe it was my childhood, where I was bullied so badly when I was growing up. I didn't think that it affected me, but looking back, it did.

"I would say it's important to have somebody that will help you through that. There are programs and tools available online. There are tons of self-help books. You will get to the point of discomfort while you are working through it. On the other side of that really uncomfortable feeling is the most amazing breakthrough.

"We typically don't like to go there because we want to protect ourselves. We don't want to feel something that's not a good feeling. I kick fear in the face now, because in every experience I've seen, like, amazing things on the other side of those fears, so I think it's important for women to form community.

"If a lady doesn't want to specifically work with a mentor, join a Mastermind group. Having the support of someone around to bounce ideas off of during a struggle, it is beneficial. They can go to that person and speak to them about what they're going through, because that's truly the only way to get it out to the world and be able to release those beliefs.

"When I was living in fear and I started working with a mentor, I started compiling a gratitude list. I am a huge believer in energy, so I believe everything in life is energy, and that we have all the tools that it takes necessary to get from point A to point B. So I practice, and I still do this daily: I go through, when I brush my teeth in the morning—or you can do it whenever—I go through a list of the things that I'm the most grateful for. This practice grounds me and it sets my intentions for the day.

"So regardless of where you are in your life or in your business, even if things are not going your way, there are still so many things that you can be grateful for. In turn, when you start building that list of the things that you're most grateful for, the world will start giving you more of that.

"I would say a gratitude list is a big, easy thing that people can implement into their lives. I mean, it is very easy for me. I do it in the morning when I brush my teeth. It can be things as simple as, 'I am grateful for this toothbrush right now.' Sometimes you're at a point where that's all you can think of, and that's okay.

"And then, as I mentioned, find a community that works for you. Find a group of women that you can bounce ideas off of, whether it is a Mastermind group, joining Success Society, or listening to Empowering Women Radio. Find that thing that you can go to and get inspired.

"For me, I think it's important. In my own life, we're busy entrepreneurs. But I also had to learn how to make time for self-care. So the first year in my business, I lacked that greatly. That was one of the things that contributed to the burnout and the resentment. I basically started resenting my own business, and that is not a place you want to be. Take time for you. Find whatever it is that you really love to do.

"Like, typically, I always take Sundays off and I have my day. If I want to go to the beach or I want to hang out with my friends or go to brunch, whatever it is, I do it, because I deserve it, because I'm celebrating myself. And then I get right back, and I'm completely fueled for the week going forward.

"The quote that I always go back to is, 'Dreams really do come true when you have the courage to pursue them,' and when you find the thing or the things that you love so much in life, never, ever give up.

"A year ago, this thought that I had for this bigger picture and this bigger vision... it was just a thought. It would have just laid in my mind as a thought, and I would have kept moving on, but I took the universe's signs, and I put them into play. My life and my business have changed drastically, even in the last few months since we've launched. So when you believe something and when you're getting these signs, I say go with the feeling. Find your success."

Cynthia Bazin:
SmartChic

Cynthia is fabulous and smart. She really connects with people on a deep level, and she's always quick to ask what she can do to support other women. She explained, "I love partnering up and talking with people who empower other women. My company, SmartChic, is all about empowering women. It's a premiere mentoring company for successful, smart women that may be stuck in one or more areas of their life. SmartChic does individual mentoring and group programs to get women really laser-focused on what their real mission is in life. This way, they can achieve really authentic success and happiness.

"I have learned a lot through the years. What success was to me two decades ago and what it is today is much different. Success, to me, is doing what makes me happy. Years ago, I was trying to live up to expectations of what others might think and what they wanted me to do. Through learning, growing, and going through the corporate world for 20 years, now I own my business. I'm at a place that I feel successful because I'm doing what makes me happy, not what others think that I should do with my life.

"It's been a growing process. I went through a lot of experiences to get to the point where I can mentor women. But I think to really find that real true success, you have to surround yourself with amazing, positive people who are going to constantly push you to do what makes you happy in life. You have to have great resources. Find inspiring things to read. Seek out friendships with people that you look up to. It's really about getting clear about what makes you happy and what your values are.

"I think we all have stumbling blocks along the way. I started out in the corporate world; my actual background is in investigations and security. I ran investigations for the last 20 years for different organizations. I worked really hard. When I was young, I felt success was working hard, working more, and throwing myself into being a total career woman. For 20 years, it was pretty typical for me to work 13–14 hour days.

"Fortunately, I had some great mentors while I was working in the corporate world, and they would say things like, 'You know what? You'd be great running your own business,' and 'You're working really hard for somebody else when you could be doing it for yourself.'

"I learned from them, and then I came into my own with my business. Along the way, I learned … that you don't have to work 14, 15, 16 hours a day. Working harder doesn't necessarily mean that you're successful.

"It's finding ways to work smarter so that you have a personal life that you can really enjoy. Work isn't everything. Now that I have learned this lesson, I have a lot more free time on my hands. I work really smart versus working hard. That's what I teach in my mentoring programs.

"Now that I am a woman entrepreneur as opposed to being in the corporate sector, I can set my own time to work. If you want to create the life that you dream of, determine the lifestyle you want. Figure out what hours you want to work and be really committed to that. For example, one of the things I always wanted to do was a three-day weekend, and I couldn't do that in the corporate world. Now I block off that time.

"You need to commit to making that time for yourself. Exercise, health, and wellness are huge things for me. I probably didn't have as much time back then, but now, I have much more leisure time! I spend more time with family, at sports functions, going out to dinner, and hanging out with friends. You just need to change the things that weren't really quite working for you.

"I've been in business for myself for almost four years now, and I've learned a lot over the last couple of years. And I will give you the straight talk as far as what I've learned. Because you know what? I'll admit I made some mistakes in the beginning—what I didn't think were mistakes—but now I've gotten much smarter and so much more successful, and these are really the keys of turning your passion into a successful business.

"First of all, don't try to do too many things in your business. There's something called the 'brilliant idea syndrome.' We've got all these amazing things we want to do with our business: we want to write a book, offer products, individual coaching, and then conduct seminars. You want to go do a million things. I started like that and wasn't really being that successful in any of them because I didn't have laser focus on a few things.

"The second problem is believing that your business is for absolutely everybody. Getting really clear on who your ideal client is and really focusing in on them is important.

"To be really successful, number one, really get laser-focused into what you're really an expert at and what your true passion is. And, number two, whether it's your marketing or speaking engagements, any sort of thing to get your business out there. Determine who your target market or your ideal client demographic. Women? Men? Age bracket? Where are they? And make sure that you are where those people are, either in social media or in person.

"You must have confidence in succeeding with your business. I really encourage people to talk about your idea. People who you feel are your ideal client... ask them what they think about your business idea, and really learn and grow. Take everybody's feedback so that you can gain that confidence in order to really start a business and grow in it.

"The bottom line is that not every single idea that you come up with is going to be successful. So don't be fearful of mistakes and things that are going to happen. Some of the most successful people in the world have had... things that haven't quite worked out. Basically, you learn from what ever went wrong.

"What are you going to do with that if something doesn't work out? You can't get down on yourself. You have to take what doesn't work, re-adjust, learn, and do it better the next time.

"Be a person of action. You have to be someone that's a little bit thick-skinned. Pick yourself up and move forward.

"I really felt that I was rocking my business when I started doing what I'm truly passionate about. You know what I mean? I'm not focusing in on stuff that I'm not good at.

"When I first started in my business, I tried to do everything. For example, my expertise is talking with people, and I want to get out there and talk to new clients. There's everything from web pages to designing email templates to social media and stuff like that. When you are trying to do everything, it doesn't feel like you are truly running a business; it feels really more like grind work.

"Work smarter. Start delegating out and eliminating stuff that you aren't good at. Start really focusing in on what you're really an expert at and gaining clientele. I think that's when you start feeling like you aren't just putting in the hours… you are running a real business.

"That was the turning point for me. I realized I'm not good at website building, I'm not a techie; I'm going to delegate that out to someone who loves it and does that well. I'm going to focus on doing my thing. Then I felt like I was in the groove and I'm a real business owner now.

"Yes, in the beginning, you have to try and do everything because of limited resources and finances. Yet, as soon as you can, delegate out what you're not good at and focus in on your real gifts.

"I think that everybody needs a mentor! I am a mentor, and I have a mentor. It's so important for all of us to surround ourselves with informal mentors and formalized mentor relationships. You really need to be with positive people, people who have walked-the-walk. Honestly, hang around with people who are smarter than you are! You don't know everything. To learn and grow through life personally and professionally, surround yourself with people who can give you that positive push to help you really go for it.

"Mentoring is so important. Not only for a sounding board. Sometimes it's rapport, and other times they provide inspiration. It can get you where you want to be in a much straighter line. A lot of people I know—and even myself, during times in my life—we have taken a kind of a curvy road to go through business and life in general. With the right mentors and relationships, you can get to places so much quicker and be inspired along the way.

"I had great mentors in my life that I was fortunate to have, and I started my business because sometimes— women, men, it doesn't matter—we feel all alone, and it's so important to reach out for support. My mission is really to help empower women and to really be able to get them to where they want to be quicker. Life is short! We have to really enjoy life, and I want women to get to where they want to be.

"I say this to women all the time, 'You are amazing and beautiful. You're strong. Life is short. Any mistakes you might have made in the past, we all make them, and you need to leave them in the past. It is what you're going to do today in moving forward that counts.

"Start doing today what makes you happy. Stop worrying about what everybody else wants you to do you only have one life. Start today and take steps towards what authentic success and happiness looks like for you.'"

Debbie Silverman:
Consumer Perspective

Debbie Silverman is a Human Behavior Specialist and the President of Consumer-Perspective, LLC, a market research and strategic planning company. She is also a neurolinguistic programming (NLP) practitioner with a degree in psychology. She has had countless conversations over the past 30 years with her clients' customers and employees.

Debbie explained what she does to help others: "Through the research I conducted, I helped clients raise the bar on how they communicate with their customers. The insights learned from these conversations created new businesses, revitalized tired brands, and converted prospects into raving fans. I live an abundant life through spirituality and gratitude for my family, friends, and business associates.

"In my book, *It's Just a Conversation*, my co-author and I offer our readers very real and poignant challenges, tips, and solutions to everyday conversations. Our readers have coined our book "the new business Bible.""

"Successful communication in business and relationships is based on our ability to F.O.C.U.S. We use the word F.O.C.U.S. as an acronym. F: Finish first (have a goal in mind of how you want the conversation to go); O: Observe (e.g., body language, facial expressions); C: Clarify (ask questions) and remain calm; U: Unique (be yourself); and S: Stay in the moment (listen and be present).

Debbie Silverman explained why women, on average, still earn 22% less than men, saying, "I contend these women earn less because they don't know how to ask for what they want and get it. Knowing how to have the money conversation, whether it's about asking for a raise, interviewing for a job, making a sale, or negotiating business deals—it is a key ingredient in empowerment.

"I asked Trish Carr to be my co-author because I knew that our readers would benefit from her sales, marketing, and networking expertise, and her experiences in the corporate world. When I first approached Trish, she was very excited about the book.

"About halfway through the process, she decided she didn't want to work on it anymore. Quitting was not an option. I reminded her of the vision I had, which was to empower women (and men) in the workforce (and everyday life) to have the conversation they want and need to have for their success.

"I asked her to imagine how it would feel if we could help just one woman gain the confidence she needs to have that conversation to ask for what she wants and see her transformation. We pictured the lady's smile and pure excitement when she got it!

"Once the book was finished, we worked closely marketing and creating the tools to get our book on Amazon. The first day we introduced it on Kindle, it became number one seller. A few months later, our publisher told us that we were number one on Amazon. We have also been recognized as an International Book Award finalist in Business and P.R. To further empower women, we created a 4-module digital sales training program that is available on our book's website, ItsJustAConversation.com.

Debbie addressed three types of personalities and how they communicate. I asked her to give strategies for the shy girl, the bossy lady, and the overly worried woman. She said, "One thing all three personality types have in common is that their unspoken conversation or their body language and facial expressions speak volumes.

The shy girl:

"The tip I would offer for this personality type is to smile (even if you don't want to). She will likely walk in a room and sit or go off to the corner by herself. Keep your arms open (don't cross them over your body), stand up straight (don't slouch), keep your head up, and make eye contact. People are attracted to a warm, friendly smile."

For the bossy lady:

"The tip for this person is to smile and to listen more. While the bossy lady may be in a tight time crunch to get something done, she will make herself more approachable (and seem less bossy) if she spends time listening. A key way to listen more intently is to lean into the conversation. Also, refrain from rolling your eyes and/or looking at your watch like you are bored. This will communicate to the employee that you are truly interested in what she has to say."

For the overly worried woman:

"The tips for this woman are to smile, make eye contact, and do not fidget (play with hair or wring your hands). Also, being prepared for the situation and conversation(s) is a good way to calm you from the worry or fear that could be paralyzing."

Debbie added, "A fun mind exercise (NLP technique) is to confuse yourself. When the mind is confused, it lets go of the troubling issue and allows you to be more creative. Here's an example of this mind exercise. Let's say you're worried about asking for a raise. Ask yourself these questions very quickly: What would happen if I asked for a raise? What would happen if I didn't ask for a raise? What wouldn't happen if I asked for a raise? What wouldn't happen if I didn't ask for a raise? (By the way, don't 'worry' if you can't answer all these questions. No one can!)

"Remember that to get more out of life, you have to ask for what you want. Don't be afraid to ask! When you ask, ask largely!"

Chapter 8:

Collaboration, Not Competition

"Clawing her way to the top." This is, sadly, how some women achieve success. At times, this is simply perception; at other times, it is a figurative way of saying that a woman is catty in her approach to making it in life.

Women, when collaborating, can create even more amazing work than they can solo. I recall being a young child, peering around the corner to see my mother and women friends in her writing group, blissfully bouncing ideas off each other. They would toss words around like it was sport and jot down responses to writing prompts. I was always shooed out of the room so that they could have their adult discussions.

I know though that there was magic going on in that room. Bubbling up in the cauldron of collaboration, they cast spells on their words and gave them life. Make your own magic together with other ladies.

Debra Dion Krischke:
Glass Slipper Ball and Inspired Women

I love the moment when each Inspired Women reveals the winner of our quarterly charitable gift. Debra Dion Krischke thinks big, and she said, "Imagine how we'll feel when we are raising $10,000 in one hour. I'm positioned to help anyone in any city launch a chapter of Inspiring Women. This is my way of paying it forward. It's all about raising lots of money for women's issues locally and internationally.

"Inspired Women: Paying it Forward is fast philanthropy at its best where members nominate their favorite local or international women's non-profit. 100% of our collective donation goes to the selected women's charity at one-hour, quarterly, networking meetings with a purpose. We all write a check for the chosen charities for $100, and from there... we make funding happen! Together with groups of friends and colleagues, we are creating space for women who have more in their lives to take action on behalf of women who have less."

Debra has perfected the art of fundraising, and choses to do it now with women that she knows share her ideals. As a social entrepreneur, Debra Dion Krischke organizes the Glass Slipper Balls, which have raised over $1 million for women charities. She has also spearheaded the Inspiring Women conferences.

One day, during a lunch meeting with me, she stated that because of our values and commitment to women, it was like she was looking at a younger version of herself.

As we chatted that day, I learned that she had dealt with the struggles of requiring payments for services rendered because she was working in a field of giving. In her move from volunteer to paid professional, she got the most pushback from the ladies.

Debra explained what she experienced: "You'd think that when you are discussing this with professional women that they would absolutely one hundred percent across the board get that, but really, what I did learn is that not everybody gets your vision when you get it. Sometimes it takes some people a really long time, and others just don't get it at all. You kind of just have to move forward, knowing what your own truth is, and hopefully they'll catch up.

"I don't believe in exploiting women in third-world countries, and I don't believe in exploiting women here at home. I counsel women all the time about having to negotiate a raise and how to better themselves and their careers. I had to do it for myself, so I know from where I speak."

It was during this this switch from volunteer to a more entrepreneurial venture that Debra discovered from where this underlying tension may arise: "Dealing with women, I have found that sometimes women don't realize that they can collaborate (they don't have to compete). This is really just something that they have to evolve into realizing: that we all just need to reach back and lift someone else up along with us. I still have found that women can be competitive and jealous, and I think that maybe they just haven't been players long enough to recognize that they don't have to worry about who's coming up behind them — they can actually reach back and lift up others.

"I have come to the conclusion that, basically, if we're alive, we need help. People don't ask for it, especially businesswomen. I think everyone's out there trying to recreate the wheel. It's not necessary. You don't have to do it alone. I think that probably one of the most important things is to look where you can collaborate, and do that — because when you're in a creative bubble by yourself, sometimes your self-talk might not be accurate. So, it's really good to either have a coach or someone that you can bounce your ideas off of. I'm a real believer in collaboration."

Debra discussed her experience living in Iran on Empowering Women Radio: "I saw a little girl that was playing on a teeter-totter, one of those see-saw things on the playground. She had a veil on and she was trying to hold the veil in her teeth... and I mean a full-length veil. They call it a 'chador' in Iran; that's a full-length veil. It's not a burka; a burka is the one that has the screen over the eyes, which really physically impairs you—you cannot see well, out of a burka.

"In Iran, they wear chadors. It's a full-length veil; their face can be open, but often times, they'll hold it in their teeth or partially cover the lower part of their face. So, this little girl was trying to play and hold this in her teeth. I just watched her, and it broke my heart then, but it was just an image that stayed with me.

"As the years went on, life went on, and I got involved in different chapters of my life. When it came time that I was able to refocus on my passion for women's initiatives, the plight of the women in the Middle East obviously was there with me organically. I had an opportunity to be in a book called *Fearless Women, Fearless Wisdom*; it's a photography book out of California. She has a whole Fearless Women's series.

"Mary Ann Halpin was the photographer. I had met her at a conference and she had taken my portrait one year with a sword, which is one of her signature items. The next year, I was at the conference and I went out specifically because I had this picture in my head. I wanted to see a woman under a burka with just a sword. I just wanted this photograph; I didn't even know where it was going or what I was going to do with it, but I wanted this portrait. I took the burka with me and I talked to her out there, and she took this portrait. It's powerful.

"When you see it, all you see is this figure under black, with her hands embracing this huge sword. I didn't know then, and I'm still not exactly sure where it's going to go and how it's going to be used, but when I have an opportunity to put that in her book, at first I was thinking, 'Well, yeah, she wants to use my portrait,' and then I started thinking about it, and I said, 'I don't want my portrait in a book; I want the woman under a burka, called Women Under Veil.' I asked her if we could do that, and she said 'Yeah!' and I said, 'Okay! Then let's do that, and I'll write my page about women in the Middle East and the kind of oppression that they have to deal with on a daily basis.'

"Then we developed a website, which I really haven't done anything with yet. It's called The Burka Project. I do have video of American women trying on this burka and what they feel like when they take it off. I put that video on this website, and I still don't know where it's all going, trust me... I have no idea.

"You know, luck is what happens when preparation meets opportunity. It's built. It's there. It's live, so people can look at it and they can see. I introduce it at every single one of my conferences, if for nothing more than to have some solidarity with women that don't live in a free land.

"I think that it's up to all of us who live in America and this place of abundance to at least have some solidarity and some compassion and understanding for what that would be like. It's going to be up to us to try to assist them. It's very difficult in enslavement like that, to get out of it. I think that more action here by women that are in a free culture is what's needed.

"Basically, every woman I have met has a story, but some of them just have a more compelling one. Some of the women I have met have overcome amazing things, and experienced triumphs in their life. When we read about women, it's inspiring. When we read about their stories and the adversity they've overcome, there's always take-aways from every story. We don't live long enough to make all the mistakes ourselves; we've got to learn from other people.

Debra further explains about books like the one you are currently reading: "It's a great opportunity for personal growth, to learn from other people's mistakes and to feel inspired, because let's face it: no matter what your story is, someone else is in a more difficult situation.

"I think an empowered woman is one who recognizes their God-given talents. I always say, 'Your life is God's gift to you, and what you make of it is your gift to God.'

"An empowered woman is someone who has enough years under her to understand what her talent is, what her uniqueness is, has to move forward with that and is able to move forward in that. I think as women, we spend an awful lot of years and decades underplaying... and undervaluing what we have to offer, and being afraid or either not being liked or what people might say. I think there's a fear there. It is beautiful once you get to the point where you just say, 'I know my own truth. I will move forward with what I think is important.'"

Maggie Delany:

Entrepreneur and Professional Network

I met Maggie Delany at the Entrepreneur and Professional Network Triple Launch Party in N.Y.C. Collaborating with two incredible businesswomen, we introduced our latest ventures to media world on the red carpet. I proudly unveiled my TV show Inspiring Lives with Dr. Shellie.

The mood was electric, with models working the runway in couture fashions, cameras flashing pictures, and women's charities being showcased and supported. I was delighted to chat with Maggie Delany for E.W. because she balances her marriage and professional life so well. She is principal of a school by day, runs the Entrepreneur and Professional Network in N.Y.C., and also owns a yachting company and a fashion line.

Maggie and I share the juggling of multiple lives from education to business owner and the red carpet life. She shared with me this principle she lives by: "Do not let society define you. You can be whatever you want to be; you just have to follow your passion and give it your best."

Maggie stated, "Shellie, I get the same reaction that you do because when people hear that I'm a principal. They are like, 'Really?' First of all, I always remind them I am a modern-day principal. It's all about breaking barriers and breaking stereotypes. When I meet with young ladies, I tell them you can be whatever you want to be. Just pursue your goals. If you do want to be a principal, go ahead. If you want to be an actress, you go ahead; you just do it. You can be both.

"I became the principal of a school in Yonkers for the past seven years. We have 640 students and I manage 89 employees. After a full day of this, people would think that I would be all exhausted... but no, no, no. When I leave my building, I take my principal hat off and I am the networker, the entrepreneur, and I keep going on. That's what really keeps me going, and I have a really supportive husband."

Maggie has a very passionate marriage with her husband. She explained, "It's really been quite a wonderful 10 years with him, but this in my second marriage. My former marriage was not a happy one, so we will not visit that. In my husband Hubert, I found the ideal man for me. I had been looking for someone who is supportive, someone who is not intimidated by what I do, and who is really always there for me. I really treasure the day that I met him. So, yes, I'm very lucky."

She recalled the night that she met Hubert: "I was very depressed because I was going through my divorce and I did not want to go out. I'll never forget that my sister said, 'Maggie, you have to get out of the house,' and she traveled from Maryland to accompany me because I did not want to go. That's why I believe in destiny. That's the night that I met Hubert. I found out that Hubert did not want to leave his house, either; he did not want to go out that night.

"Do not stay indoors and just cry; you have to go out there because you never know. Whether it's jogging or whether it's having dinner with a friend, that special person can be just about anywhere. Don't get depressed. Turn the page and move on."

Relationships are important to business and soul growth. Maggie's home foundation is strong and she believes in the power of connections in business as well, frequently networking entrepreneurs together.

Maggie described the types of women that she helps connect: "Within the women entrepreneurs, you have a very eclectic group of ladies. But more importantly, women know that they have to go the extra mile. Having worked with several women that have different personalities, I know they are surely go-getters.

"Once they have something set on their mind, on a goal, they go after it. That's what makes my work worthwhile with women. I see the passion in their eyes and they want to do it. They are ready to do it. It's been a great adventure."

Maggie explained that the difficulty with bonding powerful ladies together is, "The world looks at women as being catty or jealous or being competitive. The message that I always send is that there are always opportunities for everyone. It's a matter of collaborating and understanding, because misunderstanding can cause a lot of unnecessary conflict. I always encourage the women: 'If there is something that you are not clear about, ask questions. Don't ever hesitate to reach out.' It is so important.

"Do not take anything negative that's been said and just ponder, letting it boil inside you without reaching out to the other person. I think that is the biggest issue is when dealing with women who usually feel that 'maybe this person does not like me, or this person thinks of me this way.'

"I always tell women you have to bypass the gossip. You have to bypass other people's negative thoughts and opinions, and just move forward and just try not to burn bridges. If you can mend bridges, that's very important. There are times there is nothing that you can do because it is not a two-way street. I always tell the women, 'Don't take anything personally, and just keep moving forward.'"

Carol Evans:

Working Mother Magazine

Carol Evans is the C.E.O. of Working Mother Media and she is one of my role models. She has appeared on major talk shows including The Early Show, The Today Show, Oprah, Good Morning America, as well as on hundreds of radio shows and interviews in newspapers nationwide. Carol loves to tell the world how working mothers work to keep their families and their businesses moving and growing.

I met her when I went to Senator Kristen Gillibrand's Women's Economic Summit N.Y.U. She was keynoting and she was just a dynamo! I could see and feel all this positive energy radiating from Carol Evans. I was delighted to get to know her and to interview her for Empowering Women Radio.

Carol Evans explained her history of working as a feminist and C.E.O.: "I have been associated with Working

Mother since its very first issue of *Working Mother Magazine*. There was an idea to launch a magazine—a test, actually, of a magazine for working mothers. There was nothing like it in the world, and I was part of the team that launched these test issues, and I was in sales. I sold the most advertising into the issue. That was it for me! I was off and running!

"I was 27 years old and I was very excited about the concept, because my mother had gone back to work when I was 12. I've been a feminist my whole life, so I was thrilled to do something different from the usual women's magazines.

"I took over the management of the magazine because of my success on the sales side, and I grew it for the first 10 years of its life, launching, in 1986, 'The Working Mother's: Best Companies,' which has been a huge success all these years.

"And then, after about 10 years at the magazine, I left to go work for some entrepreneurial companies because I wanted to learn how to be an entrepreneur. In 2001, I came back and bought Working Mother from its third male owner and became the first mom to own the magazine and to run it.

"So that's been my journey since then. I have been growing, developing, and nurturing this very special place. It is a community that working mothers have in the universe to go for comfort, inspiration, and for knowledge.

"Everybody wants to be a great mom, and they want to be really great employees. We all have this yearning. Nobody wants to just be mediocre. Knowing that we have that dual strong desire, to be great at whatever we do, we have to recognize that we do put a lot of pressure on ourselves.

"But if we follow our own internal signals and really make choices that are right for us, we will end up in a very good place, as long as we stay positive about those choices. I think the worst thing that a working mother can do is to constantly doubt herself, yet I know that millions of working mothers doubt themselves all the time.

"I counsel all of our readers and our web audience to really take the positive side and make that choice, but stick by your choice and be happy with it. If it's not making you happy, then you should re-examine it.

"One thing we know for sure is that children are happy if their mothers are happy. So, if your career is inspiring you, giving you energy, and making you feel safe and secure, then that is the thing to focus on. If your career is making you feel very negative, then stop and re-examine it, but reframe your daily thinking about your career.

"This is not a world where we need to be wallowing in guilt anymore about working. We are making strong, positive choices, and the reality is that this can be such a great lifestyle for women all around the world for so many reasons.

"It was important to determine which companies are the best fits to suit the needs of a mother; that's why we created the '100 Best Companies for Working Mothers.' One of the ways we influence companies is by really examining what they offer before we take our jobs there. Then we vote with our feet by leaving if we're not satisfied.

"What every mother and every woman should be looking for is a culture of 'flex'. At different times of your life, flexibility will become extremely important. It could be that it's because you've just had a baby, or ... your child is having some trouble at school, or ... your parents or in-laws are aging. Whatever the situation, even just for your own ability to take care of yourself and your health, flexible work arrangements are key to being a best working company.

"There are other things that are so important, too, such as, is there a way to help you take care of your childcare needs? What are the health and wellness benefits? Women tend to put ourselves last, so we need to be sure that there are support systems for health. Companies should care about our health and welfare, our wellbeing.

"Those are the things to look for. Of course, you always want to make sure you are working for a company that 'gets' women and that really supports women. It should have programs and policies that really support the advancement of women within their own company.

"These are some of the key points to look for. No company has everything, but you should be looking carefully at what their policies are. Don't be afraid to ask, 'What is your maternity leave policy?' and 'Do you have paternity leave?' Ask these questions and you will really go in armed with the values you are looking for.

"When I came back to Working Mother in 2002 and bought the company, while I realized that while we had made progress in the years while I was running other businesses, still, there was so much progress to be made. It was apparent that women of color were, in so many ways, disadvantaged compared to Caucasian women.

"So, I launched an initiative right out of the gate when I first came back to Working Mother. The initiative is to support the advancement of women of color by using the same methodology that we had used with the 100 best companies to support working mothers all those years.

"When you get the attention of companies who are employing millions of women, and you tell them, 'This is how we are measuring you. This is what matters,' that really creates progress. Those companies create new policies faster and they pay attention to what's being measured.

"So, in 2002, we launched 'The Best Companies for Women of Color,' and it's been an ongoing initiative with all the research capabilities that we have. I see how multicultural women have so much to offer to companies, and yet companies don't even realize sometimes how they are disadvantaging their multicultural female employees.

"When you bring together the ideas of the advancement of women with the specific needs of women of color, it's powerful! Just bringing up the topic sometimes makes people look around and say, 'Oh yeah, we haven't looked at that.' Then you give them data on how they are doing. You show them how they can do better. Then they start building programs and policies that will really help in this arena.

"I'm excited about this initiative. It's been challenging as a white woman myself. The challenge is in really understanding and growing this initiative in a way that's authentic and helpful. I've done it only by having great partners. Women of every race and every ethnicity have come in with Working Mother Media to push this initiative forward.

"I feel that a 'feminist' is anyone who cares about the advancement of women; a person who believes that women should be equal to men with equal opportunity and equal pay. Whether they agree to the word 'feminist' or not, they believe that women should not be disadvantaged in marriage, in work, in community, in family life, and in education.

"The world is full of unannounced feminists! It's an old word that is new again, which I just love. People are like, 'Oh really, I'm a feminist?' Young women now understand that they are feminists. That's going to create a lot of energy for women around the whole world.

"My favorite charity that I work on is March of Dimes. The President of March of Dimes came to see me around twelve years ago in my role as C.E.O. of Working Mother Media. She wanted to get some media attention for March of Dimes. They were working on their biggest initiative, which is now their main focus: the prevention of premature birth.

"Well, she didn't know that my son was born six weeks early and almost died because of his lack of being able to breathe. My son's life was saved by some research they had done on the use of surfactant in premature births. I was like, 'Whatever you need. Whatever you want. I'm yours!'

"The President of March of Dimes asked me a couple of years later to join the National Board of Trustees, so I've been working with this amazing organization. The March of Dimes people are the ones that solved Polio, they got the vaccine to the world, and now they are working on the research to find the cause and create the prevention of premature birth all around the globe. It's such exciting work! It's heavy-duty research work that requires such special fundraising, which I've been a privileged person to be able to support.

"We actually decided to create a group here called The Working Mother Research Institute, to be able to devote more time to our research. We launched that about six years ago, and it's been extremely helpful. The research we do is very expensive, very detailed, and kind of grueling for the companies to go through.

"Then we do research, which is really a lot of fun, like what are ideas that working moms, women, and women of color have, and we report on those. Then we do also some research that are specialty issues for women, such as 'breadwinning moms'—we just did a whole research project on how men use flex scheduling at work, so that we can get men in on all of our ideas as well.

"We have a broad range of research that we do, whether it's about companies or about women in this country, women in different countries. It is helpful because having the data tells you the story. You know what the story is, but until you see the data points, you can't really say that this is a story that you can stand behind 100%.

"We do executive summaries of every piece of research we do, and they are all on our WorkingMother.com website. And if students or authors need more data points (because they can use this research in their own work), then they can email us—it's all on the website—and say that they'd like even more information.

"When I wrote the book, *This is How We Do It: The Working Mothers' Manifesto* in 2006, I wanted women to realize that they are not alone. That is so important; people feel like, 'I'm the only one dealing with this.' Secondly, I want them to understand that it is okay to ask for help. They may need to say, 'Hey, I need help from my husband, my co-workers, my boss, my community.' Asking for help is key.

"Also, understanding that that there's so much joy in being a working mother. You just have to reframe your thinking. This is not just about work. This is about a new lifestyle that is really only decades old. It is a lifestyle of working mothers. And we are instituting all around the world as a new standard for women.

"Feel the power of that, being part of that movement, being able to be a mom. You can be great mom and also being able to contribute in such an important way in your career, company, or your university. The joy is that in something that is so infused in the book. But also, it offers practical solutions that everybody needs, just like the magazine.

"One of my great joys and privileges in life is to be able to travel around the world. You know, we at Working Mother Media do conferences all the time. I have been to Shanghai, Brazil, India, France, Canada, and, of course, we are all over the United States talking to women. What I just want to share is that wherever I go, yes, we are talking to women, but mostly we are there to listen to women. The women in our audience are talking and participating.

"What inspires me and what gives me such great joy is that wherever I go around the world, it doesn't matter if it's a big huge city in China or a small town in the United States: women are on the same wavelength.

"It's hard for us to feel what a global concept this is, of women taking their place in society on an equal level with men. But, you know, when you boil it all down, that's what we are doing. We are taking our place in society, in work, in academia, in government, in home, in parenting, in schools; we are taking our equal place with men.

"Women across the globe are excited about this. They are struggling with it. Some are wondering how to do it. We are getting inspiration from each other.

"We cannot be impatient, because this is a worldwide movement of change. We must revel in our successes, talk about them, and know that the work is still ahead. Yet, together, women are doing it."

Chapter 9:

Servant Leadership

I was interviewing for the Assistant Principal job of a school for children with emotional and behavioral needs, which I ended up getting. I sat in the straight-backed chair in the executive director for the private school's office. He asked me how I would manage the school.

I said that I preferred to lead instead of manage. I knew the difference from obtaining my doctorate in Educational Leadership. I would not just organize and dictate rules. I would guide and encourage.

I knew in my heart that I was a servant leader. I live to serve the needs of others through leading them in the right direction.

Dr. April Torrence:
New Light Christian Education Center

Dr. April Torrence wowed my doctoral students in the Global Perspective course when she came back as an alum to guest lecture to my class, which she had attended in the past. April juggled a ministry while earning her doctorate in the Ph.D. program that I taught for a decade at Robert Morris University.

She explained that it was particularly hard because, "I have a special needs daughter who suffers from severe asthma and serious respiratory challenges. Life has had its twists and turns. All I know is whenever she is having an episode, everything else ceases, and she becomes my priority. There hasn't been a year that has gone by in the last ten years that she was not in Intensive Care for a period of time struggling just to breathe. Of course, my family is my first ministry. My ministry starts at home with my children.

"I have a wonderful husband who is so supportive in everything that I do. I couldn't have obtained a doctorate degree without his love and his support. Just being the soul provider for our home, that speaks volumes, so those are some of the things that help me currently and that helped me to obtain my doctorate degree.

"My first example of a servant leader is Jesus Christ. So the model has already been laid. There is a quote that I saw a few years ago that I sort of tweaked, and it became my life as a servant leader: 'We are the willing, led by our inspirations, willing to do the impossible for the incapable. We have done so much with so little for so long that we are empowered to do anything with nothing at all.'

"I think that is what servant leadership is all about. There is not much in return except for fulfillment. It's not a tangible return. It's nothing profitable. You know that you are impacting the lives of other people no matter how old or how young they are. You are there to serve.

"I am driven by deadlines and last-minute opportunity because I have so many roles that I have to balance. Typically, when something is supposed to happen, there are interferences. I do very well at blocking out distractions. A lot of people sometimes take offense to that, but I have priorities, and internally, I am driven by those priorities.

"So that means if I turn off my phone for three days, I am sorry, but I have deadlines that I have to meet. If I have to shut myself in a closet in the dark, and think... I am willing to do that. I do my best work at 3 a.m. or sitting in my garage in my car. I have to seclude myself away from everything so that I can get things done the way they should be done."

We talked about the decision to get her doctorate in the program that I have served as faculty for the last decade. Dr. Torrence explained, "I made that commitment to start in a doctoral program when my mother passed away from cancer. It was something that I needed to do to help me move forward and to help me heal and cope with that unexpected loss...

"I enrolled in the doctorate program and I was able to look at the program overview—and when I saw your name, Dr. Hipsky, it said that you would be teaching 'Schools, Families, and Community Partnerships, and I was very excited. Then I found out that there was a program change and that your class would now be the 'Global Perspective.' This was a total paradigm shift because I had never really thought internationally.

"My dissertation was focused on early childhood within our local community and within our state of P.A., but you gave me the opportunity to see globally. There are places in the world that can pour massive amounts of money into early childhood education; then there are other nations out there that are in underserved countries that are so impoverished, and they just want to opportunity to go to preschool.

"This year, the school that I led had the opportunity to connect through Skype with one of the schools that Haseena Patel works with in South Africa. It was powerful to watch the preschool students meet others in a new culture. We created the V4-Network based on this connection. In the next year, we plan to connect our young students to seven different countries!

"I credit you, Dr. Shellie Hipsky, for giving me that opportunity to see globally. I would not have even grasped this huge concept if I had not met you or had not taken your class. Now we can move forward with showing our students the world."

Dr. Mary Ann Rafoth:

Dean of the School of Education and Social Sciences at Robert Morris University

Mary Ann Rafoth is the Dean of the School of Education and Social Sciences at Robert Morris University. She was my boss in my professor position.

I asked her about being a woman in leadership positions at a high level. Dr. Rafoth responded, "It's interesting because coming from an education background, you might think that there were a lot of women in the workplace or that other women preceded me in leadership positions. That hasn't been the case throughout my career.

"Even when I started teaching school, I was in a big department. I think there were 20 or 21 faculty members, and there were only two women. The one was an older woman who had been there a long, long time. She took all the notes at the meetings because she was the only woman.

"I was a 22-year-old right out of school, and it was an interesting working experience to be the only woman often in a large group of men, even in an education setting. Most of the school psychologists in the field are women, but the trainers, the university faculty, are predominately men. So I, again, was the only woman in the department at both of the universities for many, many years...

"Then I became the department chair, as the first woman to chair the department. When I became interim dean at my previous university, and then later the dean, I was the first woman to be dean in the College of Education. I have dealt with being a leader where the people I was predominately leading were men."

We talked about leading, and Mary Ann said, "I've always felt it's not about how get them to do it, but how did you let them do it? Most of the time, people are ready to do things. Unfortunately, they haven't felt allowed, enabled, or supported."

Mary Ann reflected on mentors throughout her career: "My early mentors were definitely men. There weren't really any women, but they were male professors, male bosses who took an interest or recognized leadership capacity. Definitely, when I first became dean, there was another woman dean that became a mentor and a woman provost who I really feel mentored me in my new leadership role.

We recently began a new female mentorship program here at Robert Morris. Dr. Rafoth spoke about this: "It was one of the initiatives of our Women's Leadership Advisory Council at Robert Morris. We had a work group that looked at the research literature and best practices, and identified that to really begin to develop strong women and strong women alums and leaders, that a mentorship/leadership program was the best option. The programs were most successful when the girls had a strong faculty mentor that involved them in discipline and in research."

Mary Ann would suggest that ladies in college, "have a strong student mentor so you can talk about how to cope, get through school, and goals. Once they are in their career, a mentor who is a professional to network with is important." That's the model that RMU has set up, and Dr. Rafoth feels that the new program, "is going to be really successful. It's really important."

When I approached Mary Ann about doing an interview for Empowering Women Radio, she didn't really think she had anything unique to offer. Then she realized, "I lived through the situation where I had breast cancer and had to go through an extensive treatment while I was in a leadership role. I had to make some decisions, particularly, about how much I would share about my condition and my treatment, because I was in that leadership role.

"Especially because I had a mastectomy, I had a few male colleagues say to me, 'Oh, wow, that's really terrible. It must be awful for a woman to lose a breast.' It's like viewed as, like, an attack on your femininity or your womanhood, and it is difficult.

"There are body image issues, just like with anything else, but people think sometimes, like, it should be not talked about, as if it's something to be ashamed of when you lost a breast. Well, you know, it's nothing to be ashamed of. It's something that happened to you, and you're not less of a person or less of a woman because that happened.

"I was Interim Dean of the College of Education and Educational Technology at Indiana University of Pennsylvania, where I had worked for two decades and as a professor and department chair. They actually asked me to become permanent dean, and they did an in-house search, of which I was the only candidate.

"And so I was on my way to becoming the permanent dean. I had been in the interim position for two years while there were some transitions in the provost and president, so I had been in that leadership position. I was diagnosed in January, and it took a while to determine the extent of the cancer, but it was clear that I was going to have to have a mastectomy—a radical mastectomy. I was going to have to have chemotherapy and radiation, so it was going to be a long treatment.

"Obviously, there were going to be cosmetic issues. I was going to lose my hair. I was going to either wear a scarf or a wig. I was out of work for a day during chemo and going to radiation every morning. I know a lot of other women leaders who really did keep it quite quiet during their treatment and not tell anybody, and I think it's maybe possible if you have a lumpectomy or if you're just going to maybe just need radiation. Even then, people might think, 'Why are we not scheduling any meetings anymore before 8:30?'

"But in my position, I thought, 'There's no hiding this. It's going to be open. It's going to be obvious, and it's going to go on for, you know, six or nine months, so I've got to be above board.'

"Because we were in this leadership transition since I had been in an interim position and I hadn't been appointed dean, it really wasn't fair to them, either, not to be very frank about how sick I was.

"First, I went to the provost, who happened to be that woman provost who became a mentor for me. She had breast cancer and the treatment was not very invasive. She had a lumpectomy and then radiation. Her leadership team was the only part of the campus that was aware of her cancer.

"I went to her right away and said, 'You're not going to believe this, but I just got diagnosed with breast cancer.' And she gave me some good advice about going directly to a breast surgeon. I said right away, 'Do you want me to withdraw from the application for the dean position?' She said, 'No, absolutely not. I want you to stay.' So I said, 'All right.'

"I decided, though, in my situation, that I would just email everybody. I sent an email out to the whole college: 160 people. The email explained that I had been diagnosed with breast cancer. I was very specific. 'It's a lobular pattern in my right breast. I'm going to have to have a mastectomy.' I told them the exact schedule of chemotherapy and radiation.

"I believed that I'd be fine after I did the treatments. But there were a lot of rumors about how bad the cancer was and whether I was being not truthful.

"I experienced constant fatigue and fought nausea, mostly. And, you lose your hair. They tell you exactly, like on day 17, it will fall out. Well, it did. I chose to wear a wig. That was more about my kids, because my daughter was in high school and I was going to her graduation. I didn't want for her to feel like everyone knew she was the kid whose mother had cancer.

"I felt comfortable with the wig. In fact, it was really a cute wig. I keep trying to get my hair back to the way the wig was, but I don't think it will ever be that way. So I felt comfortable with it and proceeded on.

"Eventually, I had reconstructive surgery. That's a bigger operation, and I tried to time it because I could be more specific about the timing, so I did it during the summer. Again, I did a mass email explaining that I would be out for this time because I'm going to have reconstructive surgery.

"I didn't think that my colleagues would react like, 'Oh, wow! You just said you're getting a reconstructed breast in an email?' Because, why should I be ashamed? Why should that be something that's awkward? That's what is happening. It's nothing to be ashamed of, to have lost it or to want it back.

"In the fall, I had some difficulty with it. It built up a lot of fluid. It sprung a leak and I had to have some emergency surgery, and that caused a lot of kind of bad gossip, you know, like my breast had exploded. There, again, that's not what happened, but it was going to be fine. After all, why hide those details? That's what happened to me, and eventually, I had very successful reconstruction.

"During that time period, there was a movement in the state legislature to limit the amount of time women could be hospitalized after a mastectomy, and, basically, they wanted it to be an outpatient procedure. Believe me, it's a big enough deal that you should stay overnight.

"A number of my friends said, 'What can we do?' At the time, I had the TV and the radio station, because the media department was in my college, and then I remembered that I had a TV station here that had a pretty wide local coverage.

"One of the faculty members had a talk show that she did, kind of similar to you, Shellie. So I asked if she would you mind doing one of the IUP talk sessions on breast cancer. She said, 'Yeah, let's do it.' And so we did.

"There were two technicians as the two full-time staff that managed the TV station and ran it. They were there during the filming of it. As we were talking, I looked up at them and I could tell they were just enraptured. We ended it and the technicians said, 'That was really informative!'

"I was shown on the station a lot, and you can see it on YouTube. I don't know why people think reconstruction or breast cancer is something to be ashamed of or to keep a secret. I think it feeds into the mystique of the breast and it being the symbol of your womanhood or femininity. I know other women in leadership positions and the tendency has been to keep it completely quiet, to let no one know that you've been sick. Especially if the issue is the breast and you need surgery.

"I don't know why. I think maybe they worry that they'll be perceived as not being strong leaders. It's funny because I've had a lot of men who have worked for me have prostate issues, because you get to a certain age and that happens, and none of them have ever had any feelings about not wanting to talk to me about it. They felt very comfortable coming in and saying I'm having problems with my prostate and I'm making this decision, or do you think I should retire? Or, I'll be out. So that's good and I think women should be able to feel the same way.

"They should not feel like it's anything to be ashamed of. It is awkward but I'm okay. I still feel good about myself. I still feel good about how I look.

"It's been seven years in March since my surgery, which is the date they count from to determine you're clear. It's been quite a journey. Now it's over. It's definitely been a big part of my life, but it was really a big decision point for me as a leader about how to disclose that and how to update it.

"I remember the next year, at the opening day for my school meeting saying, 'All right, here's where I stand. I'm feeling good.' There was a moment of silence and everyone clapped. I felt really good and we just proceeded through that.

"I think it happens to many women with work-life balance decisions when you have to decide to leave a job or follow a partner or spouse. Not to follow them necessarily, but to have their position take priority. There are different times when maybe you both make decisions not to take certain positions in order to be, in similar cities or in a commuting distance.

"One thing I have found was that people worry too much about lost opportunity. Yet, I think if you have the willingness and the skill and talent, opportunity will find you."

Hena Gul:
Society for Appraisal & Women Empowerment in Rural Areas (S.A.W.E.R.A.)

I was approached by humanitarian and woman activist in Pakistan, Hena Gul, through Facebook. It was amazing to me that she had listened to the interview I conducted with Haseena Patel from South Africa and found me. She wanted to tell me her story through Empowering Women Radio I have connected her with media and activists from around the globe. The connections she has made have been a real blessing for her in an area of the world that can be isolating.

Hena explained, "Because of the Global Sisterhood, I do not feel I am alone anymore. I was eager to meet all the inspirational women of the world so I got connected with Dr. Shellie and Empowering Women Radio. Through her, I have connected with some of the greatest women in the world.

"I really love this program, as this is a really unique one. Dr. Shellie has created a space where all women can get connected easily and can express their thoughts and views like friends and sisters. I really feel proud of our friendship and to become a part of empowering women. Dr. Shellie has discovered a hidden power. There are so many women who are doing great work but nobody knew a way to connect them and tell their stories. Fortunately, Empowering Women Radio discovered us and showed the world.

"Empowering Women Radio has given me a gateway to learn more and tell my story regarding women empowerment. The women who really inspire me are those who raise their voices for our basic rights. The Global Sisterhood is a platform where every woman has respect for one another, where each one can easily express and share their life experiences.

"I am always fond of meeting great women who are doing well. It is important to me to learn from other women that how they are surviving even in critical circumstances. The Global Sisterhood gave me the opportunity to meet amazing women, to learn the facts about my sisters around the world, and to become stronger through our friendships.

"Women and girls throughout the world continue to experience violence, discrimination, inequality, and poverty. I live in Pakistan, which is officially called the Islamic Republic of Pakistan. It is a sovereign country in South Asia and its population exceeds 190 million people.

"Being a female, it has always been in the back of my mind that I could not do anything. These thoughts were kept in our mind since childhood. We see male dominance and it is ingrained that the women are just the caretakers of homes and kids.

"I live in a society where women were always denied their basic rights. We face violence and discrimination. Women here always fight for their freedom because we do not have the freedom of thought or freedom of speech. Here, women cannot go outside without a male companion.

"Around the world, women in different places are facing problems. Like Pakistan, there are some areas where still people have their own traditional way of thinking. Women are victims of their cultural practices, like: early marriages, violence, abuse, honor killing, the dowry problem, burning cases, acid attacks, and nobody can report all these cases.

"I always feel unsatisfied and uncomfortable with the system. I do not know what moment of life could bring trouble, because I am a female. I also always fight for my sisters and I for our basic rights. Thank God, my parents are very supportive and I always feel proud that I am their daughter. They supported my sisters and I. Otherwise, it would not be possible to move forward without their support even though they face a number of tragedies. I feel proud that I am always serving the needs of women under the male-dominated society and system. I want to continue my efforts.

"I always feel proud to be a daughter of my parents. I

give a big salute to my parents, especially my father who really supported all my sisters for their education and employment. Since childhood, I felt discrimination within my family and relatives. Yet, my father always gave priority and unconditional love to us. He motivated us to get education and to know about the world. I wish that every girl had parents like I have, especially the girls who face problems while getting education and a job due to the cultural norms.

"I must say that really I have never seen another person quite like my father. He honors his responsibilities very well as a family member and as a doctor. My parents supported my sisters and I while facing problems from everywhere. Because of their support, today I am able to do so much for women empowerment. I really love my parents and God bless them.

"As a humanitarian, I work to end existing patterns of violence that disrupt women's lives by ensuring rights-based laws and policies. We strive to create environments that are safe from violence. We support a broad range of comprehensive services that empower women to recover from trauma of violence and to rebuild their lives.

"I write blogs about girls' rights issues and leadership. There are a lot of restrictions in our society about girls' education and jobs. These women have no access to their basic rights.

"When it comes to female education rates, progress has been made around the world. I worked with different national and international organizations for women and children and to make sure that they get access to their basic rights. It is important to provide access to the right information.

"I always try to find out new ways to help empowering women and youth as well. We must make sure our women have a strong foundation to stand on. We must make sure that those around our women have the tools they need to encourage them to walk with integrity. Women should not be ashamed of who they are or where they come from.

"We are rising up to creating and empowering young women leaders and they will have further impact on thousands of other in communities, corporations, schools, and governments around the world.

"Before joining S.A.W.E.R.A., I volunteered with national and international organizations as a clinical psychologist for traumatized women and children who were affected due to militancy and armed conflict. This involved traveling to different affected areas of Pakistan. Yet, those hurdles could not stop my ambitions. My role there included counseling for individuals, groups, families and children.

"When I was still at school, as a 6th grade student, I found there were a lot of girls from very weak financial backgrounds, so I decided that I would take the initiative to support them in their education, so I established a group called 'Educators.' This group was set up to help provide education, school uniforms, books, and equipment free of charge to students from poverty-stricken backgrounds.

"Together with my two sisters, we founded the group and then involved friends and class colleagues. We each donated some of our pocket money for the students. The group became very popular. The teachers were very happy with our work. The group was hugely appreciated by everyone—and was referred to as 'Little Young Angels.'

"In addition, before joining S.A.W.E.R.A., I was successful in providing an educational scholarship to a girl near my house, with the collaboration of Women Worldwide Web. The scholarship recipient is from a family with six sisters and no boys. The family is so poor that they could not even afford one proper meal a day. We are currently launching an I.C.T. center with the collaboration of Women World Wide Web for minorities where 20 females are getting I.C.T. education.

"One of my childhood ambitions was to empower women. Education is a basic key to success. Through it we can empower women. Procuring education for each child, whether they are male or female, is my dream. I want to establish and promote 'Education for All' in schools and institutions.

"I also want to institute an Information Communication Technology center for girls who are really interested in being educated about computers. In a place where girls are not allowed to go to outside, today's digital world provides them with access to the rest of the world. Each one should have basic I.T. skills for our future.

"Vocational centers for those vulnerable females who do not have a male person within their family are vital as well. Some families do not have a not bread-earner and they are dependent. For them, I want to provide training for the women in skills like embroidery, sewing and stitching, handy crafts. It is time that we give them an opportunity to stand on their own feet. After being trained they may be able to support their family financially and they can become independent.

"I constantly try to find new ways to help empower women and youth. The mindset of our youth starts with the home. We will not see sustainable progress until women enjoy equal access to information and services, education, employment and political positions.

"We are living in a world where a lot of people that are scared to say what it is that they actually want and they could not express their feelings and opinions. This is the reason that they really don't get the things that they really want.

"My message for all women is to be strong. Unite more. Believe in yourselves and you can conquer the world. Do not underestimate, degrade, or be judgmental to anyone. Always give respect to each other. Together, as the Global Sisterhood, there is no doubt that the world will be ours."

Kemilembe Kanani:

Karagwe Vocational Training Development and Poverty Alleviation, K.V.D.P.A.

In 2006, Kemilembe Kanani founded an amazing non-profit organization in Tanzania, Africa. She explained to Empowering Women Radio, "The organization is called Karagwe Vocational Training Development and Poverty Alleviation, K.V.D.P.A. We strive to save children, support women empowerment, and youth development. The mission of our organization is to achieve transformation through self-help initiatives. Providing necessary assistance to orphans, youth, and needy children, widows, orphanages, foster homes, vocational training and evangelism is a major thrust.

"The vision of our organization is to realize Karagwe community, children, women and youth are actively participating to eradicate poverty. We want to see women developing and owing their property in our community."

Kemilembe, explained some of the wonderful projects they are doing in Tanzania: 1) They have a tailoring and clothing making project. 2) They provide H.I.V./A.I.D.S. prevention counseling, guidance and education. 3) Vocational training and computer training is conducted to educate. 4) Women are trained through their program to sew school uniforms and they are donated to orphans at schools in rural areas. 5) Support is provided also for women growing and cultivating vegetables. These vegetables are supplied to different schools and others just in the community at fellowship so people get proper food.

She explained that there are even programs for women growing small businesses: "Karagwe women benefit also from marketing support. Through this project, we are marketing different women projects in different countries and areas. We are very happy about this project. We have established fair trade with U.S.A. organization."

She explained the Ujamma Collective and Ruby Dawn Designs collaboration. Our friend from the Global Sisterhood Dawn Surgest who introduced me to Kemilembe, Dawn Surgest, hand-picked the beautiful fabrics when she traveled from Pittsburgh to Tanzania. I was very impressed with the beauty of this collection. This is just one of the examples of how marketing and connecting women internationally can make an impact.

Kemilembe expanded on why they are expanding their services for marketing training: "If the women sell their products, they'll get money, and that money will help them to support their community and their family. They will take their children to school. They will buy medicine, food, and some money will help to meet their other basic needs.

"Once they are producing, they are busy working. This is instead of engaging in different unhealthy behaviors like sexual intercourse, which could increase H.I.V.. They are busy producing, the product is getting to market, and they are able to create income for their families."

She reaches out to both genders to support the mission as well. "Men, if you want to support, please support women organizations. You would be supporting the whole community. When you support women, it doesn't mean it must be with money. You don't have to be rich. You just need to give from the heart." That is so beautiful and true in any language.

Chapter 10:

Gratitude

One of my favorite segments on my television show Inspiring Lives with Dr. Shellie was titled, "Gratitude-Giving." Whether we were playing with Tegu wooden block (supporting the rainforest) or tasting cookies from the Women's Bean Project (helping grow relationships for women through alternative food sources), my co-host and I had a ball.

During those few minutes, we demonstrated, tried out, or spotlighted products from around the world. We were thankful that each of the items gave back a percentage to an important non-profit charity.

Pina DeRosa:
Gratitude International

Pina DeRosa, a mindset effectiveness expert, was interviewed by Empowering Women Radio in Hollywood, right outside the Academy Awards for the Oscars. Pina explained what she does to help these harried Hollywood types: "I work with people who are tired of wrestling with their same thoughts and habits. Usually, they're really smart, capable, accomplished people who don't know how to stop that pattern or behavior that doesn't serve them. They want to end that internal battle and get consistency and results. They want to regain control once and for all.

"I work with both the conscious and the subconscious. Whether it's overwhelming self-doubt like questioning, procrastination, or wanting to achieve a particular goal, it's all that stuff that's in the way. It's like a Ferrari that's taking surface streets. It's all right, but it's not what the Ferrari is designed to ride on; it's really created to purr on the freeway or a track.

"We clear out all the filters. Everything is working properly and then we release whatever roadblocks may be there. Because oftentimes, people know that they're not living to the fullest extension of their purpose, their potential, and their vision. If they knew how to change it, they would have already changed it.

"I come in and optimize that just with a sense of perspective in both conscious and subconscious. That's what a mindset effectiveness expert is. You look at how certain people achieve results consistently, and it seems like it's easy for them; and then certain other people, sometimes there are roadblocks. It is fine.

"We can learn from the roadblocks. There's nothing to fix. There's nothing broken, but it's just like a water filter: every once in a while, it needs to be cleared out so the water can flow. It will still trickle through, but it will function better and more efficiently once it's cleared out. I identify the real issue, clear all of it out, and I get to watch them soar."

I asked Pina what her big success story is in life. She took me back to when she was 18 years old. "I moved to California. I moved to the U.S. That was 25 years ago. I came from Europe. I was born and raised in Italy, and then also raised in Switzerland. I always had this voice inside me that said, 'Go to California.' I remember hearing that message the first time when I was 10 years old, living around the Amalfi coast is where I'm from, in one of the big cities around there.

"I didn't know where California was. I was 10 years old and living in Italy. What did I know? I had to look it up. I knew it was in America somewhere, but it just seemed so far away, and that voice said, 'Go to Los Angeles.' So whether it's in an intuition, an inner voice, outer voice, whether it's a purpose... I don't know. I just feel right at home here.

"There have been obstacles, you know. You come fresh off the bus and you're 18, and you think you're invincible and the world is your oyster. It's part of being 18, but I got myself into a situation on campus. The readers should watch my Ted Talk on it, because I got myself into a bit of a challenging situation.

"From that moment on, from that first semester, I equated being healthy and fit and friendly with being in danger. It was a way to overcome the trauma I experienced. I hope that ladies will watch it there, not to be mysterious, but that way I'm not giving away the cliffhanger of what happened.

"Plus, it's free to watch Ted Talks. They're amazing! They're a really, really cool way to have a 20-minute break. It creates inspired action, which I love.

"After experiencing the trauma I discuss in the Ted Talk, I put on not just the freshman 15, but I actually put on a little over 50 pounds. Like after 180 pounds, I stopped counting.

"And over the years, when I was eating healthy, exercising, and wanting to get my body back in the shape that I knew it could be or had been, as I was losing the weight, I would get on the scale.

"Normally, women would go 'Woo-hoo!' and do a little Snoopy happy dance or a victory dance. I, however, would feel a red flag come up. I would feel like the internal dialogue was, 'Oh, shoot,' which really didn't make any sense, because if you're losing a few pounds, you would be like 'Oh, yay." But I was young, and I just knew it was there. I just didn't know what to do about it.

"It is what actually inspired me also to be a mindset effectiveness expert, because you look at the brain and you know you're only using 5% or 10% of the brain. I've always been curious like what do you do with the rest, like the 90%, 95% of the brain, the subconscious.

"How could I use the awareness that I had, knowing I want to shift this, but then also the subconscious that would really help me instead of the subconscious being the self-sabotage that created behaviors that didn't really support my weight loss. When I would notice that I had lost the weight, I would put it back on. I would do it, but then there was two decades of yo-yoing up and down.

"My recent success is that I, finally, after realizing what was going on with myself, I used my own tools onto that particular yo-yo. The reason I wasn't using them was because I thought it was handled.

"It was kind of like a forgotten box of Christmas ornaments that was packed and labeled properly, but like, dusty, you know, in the basement. I was like, 'Oh, that's what was there.'

"Now I have a different set of ways to handle life and to handle challenges versus the 18-year-old who thinks that she's in charge and she can take care of herself. Of course, society teaches us we need to be self-sufficient.

"So having regained control not just of my mind, but also my body, I went not only back to a size 4, but now to somewhere between a 0 and a 2. I feel really healthy, fit, and strong, and I have released the extra padding. Other women have been inspired, like if she can do it I can do it, because I went through so many traumas.

"I went through early menopause. I went through like all the possible challenges in the world. I had done anything and everything fitness-wise—you name it— diet-wise, whatever, that if I can do it, seriously, anybody can do it.

"It was not a predictable future for me, and it's not just the external result. It's the internal ending of that battle, once and for all, because it's draining for us. It costs us peace of mind and costs us our own effectiveness. It costs us our own way of being in the world. Peace of mind, really.

"I wrote a book about it called *Fit from the Inside Out*, and it's designed to empower men and women. I'm working with other clients who've also lost like 30 and 40 pounds, and empowering men and women to get their body back—and it's all about mindset, ultimately. I applied these lessons to fitness because it was my area of pain. But when I work with my clients, they apply it to maybe writing a book or to doubling their income or to being married and having a kid, all those things that are important to their quality of life.

"Success, I would say for me, is that inner peace. When we have a vision and we have obstacles in the way of that vision, the bigger the vision, the bigger the obstacle. Welcome to life, right?

"When we question if we should take this road or that road, then after some due diligence, we make a choice. We don't constantly question and wonder if we are doing the right thing; that, to me, is success. It is not like you need have $12 million in your bank account or you've got Oprah calling you to go on her next adventure with her. Knowing that you're on your right path: that, to me, is success.

"It is important to make a difference, give back, and utilize our challenges to help others become empowered. I mean, my purpose is to live, to learn, and to empower. Sometimes I'm doing more living. Other times, I'm doing more learning or I could be doing more empowering. I feel if I'm on all those three, then, for me, I have hit my definition of success."

Pina talked to Empowering Women Radio about the charity nearest to her heart and the documentary that's spinning off of it, which is Sniffing Out Cancer. Pina said, "I lost my best friend to cancer a few years ago. She was a bright light in the world, nearly newly married. She was super healthy, a dancer. Not a chain smoker. She was a marital and family therapist. My friend was very spiritual. She was a bright light in the world.

"A few times, she was sent home with antibiotics because she had a pain in her tummy. Well, it turns out by the time they found what it really was, it was a stage four cancer, and it was too late. She battled it as much as she could. Then, at the end, she was just tired.

"The cinematographer of my Ted Talk, Adriana, reached out to me. She's a filmmaker; she told me about her next project. Adriana said, 'I know you love conscious stuff and making a difference. I know you love dogs. Did you know that dogs can detect cancer earlier and with greater accuracy than any medical equipment out there? There are studies that are federally funded. They're published in medical journals. I researched this. There's no documentary movie about it. I don't understand why, so my next project is directing and producing this movie.'

"I replied to Adriana, asking, 'What do you need?' I watched what she had and the news clips that were available. I looked at the studies that were published in medical journals, as well as different statistics. One in three women will be affected by cancer. In America, it's one in three. Actually, for men, it's one in two."

Pina believes that Sniffing Out Cancer: The Documentary will make an impact of lives by providing awareness to the dogs and providing earlier detection for people like her dear friend.

For ladies who are dealing with obstacles in their lives, if they are experiencing blocks, Pina would say, "Not only do I see obstacles, I'm guided by them. I think it's Zen Buddhism, a saying that states, 'Pain pushes until vision pulls,' so it's really looking at pain pushes us enough until we're like, all right, enough already, and we create that vision. So what is that vision? The bigger the vision, the bigger the challenge is.

"If you have big challenges, that means you're moving. If you are not having any challenges, you're probably just sitting on the couch, watching TV with a sandwich or a bowl of popcorn. Your biggest challenge then is remembering where you put the remote.

"So when I talk to my clients and I hear that there are challenges, it's good. That means that they're moving. Just like a little kid that learns how to walk, every time they fall down, they get up. No matter how crazy bad of a parent someone might be, I've never heard of someone saying to a kid that's learning how to walk, 'Well, you keep falling down. You're a sitter. So just sit this life out and then maybe you'll walk in the next one.' It's like, well, just get up again.

"I hit several major challenges, but that tells me I'm moving. That tells me I'm growing. We all hear the word 'no' at times. As women, sometimes we feel bogged down by the 'no.' My invitation to you is to think, 'What is this yes to?' It's a yes to something else, and follow that yes. A no is not a no. Follow the yes. There is a yes behind a no. What is it a yes to? If the universe is saying no to you, if God is saying no to you, if your best friend is saying no to you, what is it a yes to? Keep following the yeses.

"Take action. Get up again and reach out. If you don't know how to get up, then reach out, whether it's to me, to Dr. Shellie, or to your best friend.

"Give back as well. I know as women, probably we give too much. Sometimes it's stopping something. Saying no is okay. It's a yes to something else. When maybe a man says no to me, maybe it was a bullet dodged. Maybe I wasn't being rejected. Maybe I was just being saved. When I say no to overscheduling something, I'm saying yes to quality of life."

Phyl Macomber:
Make A Difference, Inc.

Making a Difference isn't just the name of her company, it was a big part of how Phyl Macomber was raised. Phyl was adopted from St. Joseph's Orphanage in 1961 when she was seven weeks old. When she was a little girl, Phyl asked her mom why she and her father had adopted her. Her mother replied, "Because Daddy and I wanted to make a difference. And, when you grow up, Petunia, you will find your own unique way to make a difference in this world."

Phyl's parents taught her that no contribution was too little and that any effort to help someone counted in life. This family principle has been the driving force in Phyl's quest to better serve others in life. The name of her company being Make A Difference, Inc. not only honors both of her parents, it also recognizes the contributions of the many millions of educators and related team members around the globe who are so committed to helping the learners of our world.

As an education professor and former teacher, I know educators well. Therefore, when I met Phyl in N.Y.C. at the National Publicity Summit, I could sense that she possesses a heartfelt passion to change the lives of others by bringing her research-based, educational framework, *T.H.E. P.A.C.T.*, to the world. Phyl is determined to bridge the gap between special education and general education. She has dedicated her life to making a greater difference in education everywhere.

Since completing a fellowship at Johns Hopkins Hospital's Kennedy-Krieger Institute in 1988, Phyl has trained and consulted with literally thousands of teaching staff, successfully helping them gain control of their instruction to produce the results that they need to reach each individual child they serve—regardless of ability—along with improving the quality of their day-to-day work life.

As President of Make A Difference, Inc., Phyl has "walked-the-walk" in countless classrooms—directly teaching children of all ages, ranging in abilities from gifted to special needs—to model for teaching staff her proven strategies of meaningful inclusion in a "one-size-does-not-fit-all" methodology.

Phyl explained, "We can make a difference in the lives of women and girls internationally by teaching females around the globe not to be afraid of indicting the status quo. As the aviation pioneer, Orville Wright, once said, 'If we worked on the assumption that what is accepted as true really is true, then there would be little hope for advance.'

"Girls and women the world over should be inspired to

have the courage to challenge the existing state of affairs when the current model isn't working. They need to be vocal about calling into question that which is broken, flawed to begin with, or, in what is far too often the case, simply flat-out wrong.

"And perhaps, most significantly, the women and girls of the world need to know that they are not alone in their quest to improve their own lives, their family's lives… and the lives of others who they may touch in their journey along the road of life.

"My initial interest in the field of special education started when I was a child, growing up with my first cousin, Pam, who has a developmental disability. Pam was like a big sister to me in my large Italian family, with the two of us spending a significant amount of time together.

"I comment frequently that my family members did not treat Pam differently. In fact, when I was old enough to understand that Pam had a disability, I told my parents that, 'We were all different; no one was the same.'

"In 1988, I completed a fellowship at Johns Hopkins Hospital's Kennedy-Krieger Institute, serving as a technology specialist for both national and international referrals of special needs children and their families. The majority of my work was 'giving a voice' to non-speaking children with multiple disabilities.

"In a leadership role, I identified customized technology solutions for these children and their families to use in their education, home, and community settings around the globe. During my time at Johns Hopkins, I also trained multiple rotations of pediatric residents from all parts of the world in cutting-edge communication equipment, instructional technology, and inclusionary practices.

"After completing my fellowship at Johns Hopkins Hospital's Kennedy-Krieger Institute, I focused my work on educating and advocating for children with disabilities. In 2007, I had the opportunity to donate time to work with the ABC Extreme Makeover: Home Edition television crew for a special needs learner and his family in the state of Vermont.

"In addition to the home having complete accessibility, generator back-ups, and climate control for the child's intensive medical needs, the ABC team and I set up the technology package in the home so that this preschooler could be as independent as possible.

"I firmly believe that a child with a disability does not 'earn' her or his way into the general classroom; rather, it is that child's 'right' to be a contributing member of that classroom. My 'Phyl-osophy' of 'Education for All' is a foundational principle of my teaching framework, *T.H.E. P.A.C.T.*, highlighting the importance of accessible curriculum for learners of all abilities in an inclusionary setting.

We all have numerous things competing for our time, both in our work life and personal life. Phyl explained, "The key is to identify the most vital ones to focus on, break them down into a few simple steps, and achieve mastery. Get them 'across the finish line' in a way that is easy, yet comprehensive.

"These are some of the key foundational principles of

T.H.E. P.A.C.T. framework that I have authored: Simplify, simplify, simplify, and master, master, master.

"I have trained thousands of women in education to do a few things and do them well. I highlight the importance of the what, why, and how of their tasks, lessons, and contributions. This approach yields greater results for both teachers and the children. Yet this really applies to anything we need to do, not solely in the field of education.

"If we embrace consistency and predictability in our strategies and action plans, the tools we use for achievement become so automatic for us to implement that it reduces our brain load and things come easier to us.

"With this type of laser-focused approach, your contribution will not only be greater, but it will also be more meaningful, and the experience when making your contribution will also be significantly more rewarding for you. This, in turn, will lift you up and give you more energy and commitment to continue to contribute.

"Sharon Glennen was my mentor, in both graduate school and at Johns Hopkins Hospital. She taught me that when serving children with varying abilities, the focus should always be on the child, no matter what the politics may be or what roadblocks one may encounter. Ever since, this has been—and always will be—the ultimate litmus test that I apply to any situation in the field of education which does not seem to have a clear-cut answer or resolution.

"I am grateful that my grandmother, Phillie Scaccia, after who I am named, was a strong role model in my life. She was a beacon of strength for me, showing me the importance of always focusing on solutions rather than problems. She emphasized approaching problem-solving from a realistic, pragmatic perspective. Although she certainly encouraged me to have high ideals and far-reaching goals, my grandmother grounded me in the need to always remain practical in the pursuit of my ideals and goals.

"My cousin, Pam Polizzi, who was born with a developmental disability, taught me more about disability awareness than I learned in any academic classroom. Pam has taught me ever since our shared childhood that everyone has the ability to learn and contribute. Her "never give up" mindset has been a sterling example to me of the extreme importance of unending belief and unyielding personal commitment.

"I think that almost every person who strives to make a difference begins with two beliefs. The first is that the future can be better that the present, and the second is that they have the power to actually make it better.

"I firmly believe that each one of us can truly make a unique difference in this world. The key is to identify what your specific mission is, believe in it, and never lose sight of how it will help others. We can all be catalysts for change—significant change—if we absolutely, positively, refuse to take "no" for an answer.

"We each can ask ourselves if we want to (1) live in the world as it exists today, or (2) help create a better tomorrow that we know is possible for all of us.

"I feel that my best decisions in my own life have come from listening to my intuition and following my gut instinct. I would suggest that if you feel in your heart that you have received a call-to-action to serve, there should be no going back, because the world is waiting for your contribution... yours is an idea whose time has come."

About the Author:
Dr. Shellie Hipsky

Dr. Shellie Hipsky (www.ShellieHipsky.com) inspires, educates, and entertains internationally. For over a decade, she served as a professor at Robert Morris University and was honored by FacultyRow.com as a "Super Professor" chosen from over 100,000 professors globally.

Dr. Shellie Hipsky inspired internationally with her personal life story and the stories of the amazing people in her book *Ordinary People Extraordinary Planet*. She recently co-authored the international best seller *The Missing Piece in the Law of Attraction*. She has published hundreds of articles and her other book titles include: *Drama Discovery, Arts Alive, Differentiated Literacy and Language Arts for the Elementary Classroom, and Mentoring Magic: Pick the Card for Your Success.*

Hipsky was the Executive Producer and TV Talk show Host of "Inspiring Lives with Dr. Shellie" which was taped in an NBC studio and viewed around the world. She was deemed "Inspirational Woman of the Month" in *Inspirational Woman Magazine* and a "Luminary Author" for *Inspire Me Today*. She earned the Women's Small Business Association's "Best Business Woman" of the Year in Pittsburgh in 2013, in Washington, D.C. she earned the 2015 "Entrepreneur of the Year in Inspiration and Empowerment", and the National Association for Professional Women "VIP Woman of the Year" in 2015.

A performer and volunteer since she was a child, she is renowned locally for her acting/singing talents and utilizes them to host galas such as the Fabulous Forties which have raised over $100,000 for homeless children in shelters. Active on multiple non-profit boards, she is extremely passionate about the Homeless Children's Education Fund charity and serves on the advisory board. Dr. Shellie has been invited to present at international conferences, at Oxford University in England, and spoke to over a thousand people at Pepperdine University and keynoted the United Way Professional Connections for Women Conference.

The latest of her 8 published books the "*Common Threads* trilogy" provides *Inspiration, Empowerment,* and *Balance* based on 100 amazing interviews for Empowering Women Radio!